The Leader's Garden

Mark Tilsher

Copyright © 2022 Mark Tilsher

All rights reserved. No part of this book may be reproduced in any form by electronic or mechanical means, including in information storage and retrieval systems, without permission in writing from the publisher, except by a reviewer who may quote brief passages in a review.
This is a work of fiction. Names, characters, places, and incidents either are the product of the author's imagination or are used fictitiously. Any resemblance to actual persons, living or dead, events, or locales is entirely coincidental.

ISBN
978-1-7923-9080-7

Edited by 27:17 Editing Ministry

DEDICATION

I would like to dedicate this book to the following people:

God

I will never deserve the blessings you pour on me and only pray others see you in my work.

My Wife, Angela

No one deserves the best that life has to offer more than you do. You are the most selfless human being I have ever met, and without you, my life would be void of meaning. I will never stop endeavoring to be the man you deserve and am grateful for your patience, your support, and most of all, your love.

My Children

Justice, Kyree, Kenzie, and Kayleigh, the friendship and joy you bring make my life worth living. I am grateful to be your father and honored that God would choose your mother and me to serve as your teachers and guardians. Thank you for allowing me to practice the lessons from this book on living, breathing people.

The Chronister Family

Your impact on my life cannot be overstated. Thank you for demonstrating what a real family looks like during a critical stage of my development, without which I may have never learned what I wanted my own family to look like.

As a special thanks for purchasing my book, I would like to GIVE you a copy of the audiobook for **FREE.**

TO GET YOUR FREE COPY GO TO:
http://audiobook.leadersgarden.com

The Leaders Garden
Community

WATCH THIS VIDEO TO LEARN MORE:
http://theleadersgarden.com
&
Download the APP!

If you want to be a leader of influence but feel isolated and overwhelmed by the culture around you, then The Leaders Garden Community is for you!

Our robust community is full of like-minded leaders from various professions around the world that meet regularly for coaching groups, live Q&A sessions, book clubs, and webinars hosted by Mark Tilsher and some of the best thought leaders in the industry.

The fastest way to grow is to learn from the experiences of others, and that is what the Leaders Garden Community is all about.

Stop going through your leadership journey alone!

CONTENTS

Dedication iii
Introduction vii
CHAPTER 1 1
   If Only They Knew 1
Chapter 2 15
   We All Need Something Special 15
Chapter 3 31
   What Are You Fighting For? 31
Chapter 4 43
   Something Has to Change 43
Chapter 5 53
   It's Time 53
Chapter 6 67
   Chips & Salsa 67
Chapter 7 81
   What Do You See? 81
Chapter 8 99
   Where To? 99
Chapter 9 109
   Turn Up the Heat 109
Epilogue 124
ACKNOWLEDGMENTS 130

INTRODUCTION

"The beginning is the most important part of the work." Plato

If you are anything like me, by this point in your leadership journey, you have read dozens, if not hundreds, of leadership books and racked up ten times that many hours attending in-person courses and online webinars and watching motivational videos. Throughout all my education and experience, what sticks out to me the most is that while I can repeat philosophies on resilience, emotional intelligence, work-life balance, and mentorship, for most of my journey, I've always felt like what I've learned was worth practically nothing when it came to leading people in real life.

Like so many others, I rested on my laurels being "leadership smart," something I define as "having all the answers but no clue what to do." You may recognize this condition in a brand-new military lieutenant fresh out of the academy or a Master's graduate with a degree in economics who can't turn a profit running a lemonade stand. All too often, this mindset persists throughout a person's career and becomes a part of the leadership DNA they endeavor to pass on. Personally, for far too long, I struggled to unlock the potential of the people that mattered most to me and my organization because I lacked practical leadership tools to both implement and pass on.

In society, we tend to easily differentiate book smarts from common sense, but as far as I can tell, there is no equivalent contrast in the leadership arena. I would argue strongly that there should be. Knowing the definitions of resilience and fortitude does not prepare you to build healthy people any more than knowing the definition of leadership equips you to lead people to their performance peaks.

Herein lies the problem in my estimation: leadership legacies are forged when great leaders impart their skills, knowledge, and abilities to those they lead in a way that continues on long after they're gone. Unfortunately, most leaders I've met have no leadership legacy to follow and therefore build their legacy on trial and error.

My life's mission is to bridge the gap between head knowledge and practical application in a way that you can both learn and pass on, starting your own leadership legacy in the process. With this book, I will attempt to tackle one of the most critical challenges a leader will ever face: how to grow healthy, high-performing people and how to do our part in pulling them back when they are spiraling toward rock bottom.

My sincere hope is that this book will irreversibly change at least one person's life and possibly even save one. I know that my life was saved when a young staff sergeant, Kevin Chronister, implemented these principles in my life at a time I needed them the most.

Before we begin, I want to say that I believe human beings learn through story, which is how the bulk of our wisdom and knowledge was passed down throughout the majority of human history. Therefore, I decided to write this, my first book on leadership, in a combined fiction/non-fiction format rather than in the more traditional non-fiction route. As you read this book, you will be following our protagonist, Kevin, as he is confronted with his latent tendencies, the consequences of past decisions, and how to reconcile them with the way he lives, loves, and leads.

Special thanks to Jeremie Kubicek, Steve Cockram, and Pub House© for allowing me to use their simple visual tool, "The Pit of Despair," from which the main concepts of Time, Vision, and Encouragement are derived.

CHAPTER 1

If Only They Knew

"You never wrote me back, Kevin. You were supposed to stop at the garden center on the way home, and I'm sure you missed it. Now it's closed and there's no way for you to get the order in on time. You let us all down, Kevin. Don't bother with excuses. We get it."

The words echoed in Kevin's mind as he played the text message back to himself over and over again. He was only a few minutes from home now, and even had the weather been ideal, Kevin was driving faster than any of his neighbors would have approved of.

The windshield wipers were moving at a furious pace just to keep the road visible. Kevin had driven the roads so many times that, even in the rain, even through his anger, making the last turn towards his house could have been done by muscle memory, maybe even blindfolded.

Turning into his driveway, he hit the turn nearly at speed and drifted more than a few feet down the driveway before regaining control of the vehicle. He hardly noticed.

The Leader's Garden

Kevin had been on autopilot for the drive home and lost track of the route he had taken and how much time had passed. The only thing he registered in the moment was the pain in his fingers from the white-knuckled grip he had on the steering wheel.

He was already three hours late coming home, and now he had been sitting there for almost ten minutes, the coming conflict with his family weighing heavily on his mind. At some point, he had decided to forgo the garage, which would have alerted everyone he was home, and sit in the driveway instead. Now, the vehicle lights were splayed across the house, and the motor was still running. To anyone looking on, there was no movement, no indication that Kevin was going in the house any time soon.

The torrential downpour pounding the roof of his S-Class Mercedes felt like an external manifestation of his inner turmoil, and Kevin felt determined to let the rain stop before he got out of the car if for no reason other than to delay the coming explosion.

What a heck of a day. Kevin had found out that his best project manager and one of his star performers, Eric, had been missing work and having his subordinates cover for him. If that wasn't bad enough, Kevin had failed to stop at the garden center on the way home to place an order for a project his son Anthony was doing to earn a badge for Boy Scouts—a broken promise to add to the pile he had been accumulating at an ever-escalating rate these days.

It wasn't like he had forgotten. He had meant to do it, even budgeted his time, but that time got away from him with everything that had come up at work. His wife had texted him a reminder, which he had never gotten around to responding to, and she had even tried calling him after he was already an hour late coming home to make sure he didn't forget. But today was not Kevin's day, and they were just going to have to understand.

Had this failure been a one-off, it would have gone virtually unnoticed. Truthfully, ever since his family had agreed to start their own business, Kevin had been working longer and harder hours. It had been almost two years of bootstrapping hustling, and he was nearly as tired of it as his family was. Recently, Kevin had promoted Eric to Lead Project Manager, and he had been doing wonders to mitigate some of his day-to-day stress.

Sadly, Eric's performance had started slipping inexplicably, and Kevin had been picking up his slack, all while trying to figure out what was causing the issue. Now things seemed to be coming to a head, with Eric completely flaking out on projects and causing Kevin to miss his own commitment to his son because he had been taking Eric to task over his performance.

Still, while all of this was weighing on Kevin's mind, it felt like his family was apathetic to the load Kevin was carrying. From where he sat, all they seemed to care about was how the stress he was under impacted them. They seemed to ignore the fact that stress had been piling on Kevin at an ever-increasing rate the last two months, and all that was going to matter to them when he walked in the door was that he was about to disappoint Anthony.

Anthony had been planning his Scout project for months. He was going to be putting in a new retaining wall at their church that would expand the children's playground. He had raised the money for the project by hosting car washes and other volunteer events and had put together the itemized order for the project. All Kevin had to do was drop the order off, which he had been meaning to do all week. Today was the deadline.

Now, there was no guarantee that order would be put in on time, and all because Kevin had inadvertently waited until the last minute and missed the deadline altogether. He had broken his promise to take care of it, a broken promise only reinforced by his wife's text.

You let us all down, Kevin. Don't bother with excuses. We get it.

The words should have broken his heart, and at first, minor pains of regret crept in at the edges, almost breaking through to the center. But as fast as those feelings crept in, thoughts of how unfairly his family was treating him and how unreasonable their expectations were drowned them out. How could they not understand what he was going through and that these setbacks were only temporary?

Their warehouse automation company was growing rapidly, which was a huge blessing, but all that growth certainly brought problems of its own. Kevin had thought everyone knew things would level out soon and they could be a family again. His family just had to roll with it for a while and not kill each other. Kevin felt like they had all walked into this new business with open eyes, but now he was starting to think that he was the only one who was willing to sacrifice for the cause.

Indignation bubbled to the surface, and Kevin capitalized on the moment, exiting the car and sprinting to the door. The house was quiet when he walked in.

Julie had lit a few candles, the firelight splashing mood lighting across the walls. Barely audible classical music came through several speakers throughout the downstairs, which created a warm and welcoming environment.

Julie was an amazing woman and had been Kevin's rock throughout his adult life. She had been unwaveringly supportive, and Kevin knew she always went to great lengths to ensure their house was their refuge and peace—but these days, it seemed like she had just about hit her limit.

Kevin set his bag down, left his wet shoes and coat in the doorway, and made his way to the kitchen. There was a time, even a year ago, when Kevin would have rushed straight to greet Julie, but for the last few months, they had been fighting more and more frequently, which often had Kevin heading straight to the kitchen to check on dinner or to his home office to send a few last-minute emails.

"Anthony's upstairs in his room," Julie called to him from the dining room, forgoing any formal greeting of her own. "You got him this time."

Her voice was cold, detached, but not angry as far as Kevin could tell. While he didn't detect anger, something worse, something like disappointment lingered in her voice. If it was in him or in herself for trusting him again, he couldn't tell.

Kevin walked into the dining room to find Julie sitting in silence with a half-eaten plate of dinner. Much of his anger had cooled upon entering the house, though he still held onto his defensive posture.

"Julie, listen. I was headed straight to the garden center; I got tied up in a meeting with Eric. I didn't expect…" Kevin started to say before she cut him off.

"Stop, just stop, Kevin. We don't care about Eric. We don't care about the business. We only care about you, Kevin. We care about this family and the promises you make *us*. Did you ever stop to think that Anthony is depending on you for his Scout project? The church has volunteers showing up to help him. People have rearranged their lives for this. Do you think about anyone but yourself, Kevin?"

Kevin began to boil inside but did his best to contain it. "Of course, I do, Julie. I never meant for this to happen. I would never have done this on purpose. I had every intention—"

Julie cut him off again. "Save it, Kevin. Your son is upstairs, and he's heartbroken. This project is important to him. It was important to me that you followed through and kept your word."

Kevin offered a meager apology. "Julie, I'm sorry. I'll go to the garden center first thing in the morning and…"

Julie stopped him. "I know you are, Kevin. I'm sure it will all work out." She paused, dead air passing between them for several seconds. "You better go check on Anthony."

Kevin stared at her for a second. Part of him wanted to lash out and show her just how much pressure he was under with this family and the office. Part of him wanted to apologize and make this right. Pragmatically, however, he knew neither of those was going to work out in either of their favor, so he just took a deep breath and started his slow walk up the stairs towards Anthony's room.

Reaching Anthony's door, he raised his hand to knock.

Instead, he placed it and then his forehead on the door frame. *Why does this have to be so hard? Why can't I just walk in and apologize?*

Kevin loved his son. Even more than that, he liked him. Anthony had always been a great kid—easy to get along with, charismatic, funny, and intelligent. The two had been inseparable most of Anthony's life, but as he hit middle school, Kevin's career had picked up, and as Kevin got busier, Anthony got more distant.

Kevin stood still, paralyzed, fear sliding into his heart like a jagged shard of ice. *Has too much time passed with too much left unsaid? Am I losing my son? Can I ever get our connection back?*

Without a plan in his mind, Kevin knocked, his hand moving almost of its own volition.

"What?" Anthony's voice rang out from the other side, and Kevin couldn't help but marvel at how deep it had gotten these last few months.

"Anthony, it's Dad. Can we talk?" Kevin said firmly.

Anthony snapped, almost reflexively. "Why? I don't have anything to say to you."

Kevin replied, "C'mon Anthony, I'm sorry I let you down. I know I promised—"

Kevin was cut off again for what seemed like the hundredth time tonight. "Are you, Dad? Are you sorry? You made me a promise, and I was counting on you! You promised you would be there for me, and you weren't. You know mom said it takes at least a week to deliver custom orders this big, and today is one week. You waited until the last minute, and now I have to pay for it…"

Kevin launched into his own offense. "Anthony, I know you're upset, and I am SORRY. I said as much already. I will go first thing tomorrow morning and get this taken care of. I promise I will make it right, and you will have everything you need. I promise, son."

A long pause followed Kevin's words. Neither of them broke the silence for a moment.

"Son?" Kevin probed.

Anthony shot back, "Do whatever you want, Dad. I don't care."

Kevin stood there, dumbfounded. He stared at the closed door and opened his mouth several times but couldn't think of the right thing to say, so he just said, "Good night, son," and walked towards his bedroom, stepping into his bathroom and locking the door behind him.

Kevin was too frustrated to do anything but put his hands on the sink and alternate between looking up at himself and down at his hands. Eventually, he got the toothpaste out and started brushing his teeth. *Why does it have to be like this? They know I don't deserve this. They know this is only temporary and things will get back to normal soon. This is not as big a deal as they are making this out to be. I don't deserve to be ostracized just because things didn't go as planned. I'm doing my best.*

Kevin continued replaying everything in his mind, holding mock trials in his head as he did and declaring himself innocent of all charges every time. *Maybe they just need to be reminded of how much I sacrifice. A little perspective will do them some good.*

This went on for nearly twenty minutes before he made his way to bed, where Julie was already tucked in and waiting. Kevin took his time, walking slowly, dressing in his nightclothes and sitting on his side of the bed.

"Julie, do you want to talk about what happened?" he asked.

When she replied, it was as if she had rehearsed her words a thousand times.

Pleading with him, she said, "Kevin, I can't do this anymore. You have to fix things with Anthony. If you can't handle your work and show us that we are the most important things in your life…" Julie paused, seemingly holding back her true thoughts. When she spoke again, her words sounded much more like an ultimatum. "Kevin, I love you, but I just can't do this anymore."

She turned the light off on her last words, and the two sat in silence for a long time until Kevin heard Julie's breathing slow and was sure she was asleep. Eventually, Kevin got under the covers but struggled to fall asleep. He tossed and turned for hours until a night full of memories and nightmares welcomed him.

The muffled sounds of shouting permeated the closet door and slammed into small, 8-year-old Kevin. With each slammed door or knocked over lamp, Kevin squinched his eyes shut, praying for it to stop. Though the voices were muddled, it was impossible for Kevin to block out the words, even with his fingers in his ears

"Look at me, Michael! Don't you dare walk out," his mother yelled, while his father countered, "Why should I keep talking when you never listen?"

His father wasn't an unkind man, and he had never hit his mother or hurt Kevin, but yelling and screaming were a daily occurrence in his house. His mother and father had long ago settled like oil and vinegar; they only really came together when passionately shaken up.

The dream continued, replaying itself, even switching between ages, dates, and settings, but the actors and the themes were almost always the same.

When awake, Kevin couldn't remember much about his father, but he did remember the arguments, the yelling, and the fear he had that someday his mom and dad would split up and that somehow it would all be his fault.

In real life, his nightmare had played out just like that. His dad had left them close to his ninth birthday, and aside from the occasional birthday or Christmas card, the two of them would rarely ever see each other again.

His struggle with abandonment issues was a constant from then on, and at that moment, they manifested in his need to control situations and the emotional state of those around him. When relationships were at their worst, Kevin's nightmares would often transport him back to the time his whole world had fallen apart because of relational pressure.

Kevin woke in a cold sweat the next day, fear weighing heavily on his chest.

I'm going to lose them...

He was at the bottom of a deep, dark hole and had no idea how to start digging himself out. Something had to change.

===========The Big Idea===========

Like Kevin, many of us struggle to live out work-life balance and to care for the emotional state of ourselves and those around us. Also, like Kevin, even when we have the best intentions, life can get out of hand.

Work-life balance is one of the most significant challenges professionals face right now, and any choices we make often ripple across our families, teams, and organizations.

Sometimes, when under high stress, we fail to prioritize the biggest problems in our personal and professional lives until their symptoms make them urgent. By then, it's often too late to avoid the worst of the consequences.

When this happens, it is vital to act swiftly and identify what small steps we can take today to rapidly improve our reality and the reality of those we love most.

=========== Exercise ===========

Considering your family/team:

1. Who would you like to see the greatest relational improvements with?
2. Who needs the most attention to resolve current conflict/performance issues?
3. What would the impact be if those issues were not addressed?
4. What would the impact be if those issues were addressed?

CHAPTER 1
Reflection

"An ounce of prevention is worth a pound of cure." Benjamin Franklin

In an ideal world, our work-life balance would be under control, and all of our relationships would be on a healthy, upward trend. In the real world, however, every choice we make as leaders comes with a tradeoff, and often we choose to sacrifice that which is most important to us, believing that the long-term payoff will be in everyone's best interest.

Despite being told ad nauseum that "children grow up so fast" or "money isn't everything," we continue to fall into the same traps as our parents and their parents before them. Most of us fail to understand early enough that millions of micro-interactions form the foundations of our relationships, and these can never be replaced or undone with pep talks, vacations, or quick bouts of quality time.

Somehow, the idea of making up for neglected emotional connections with quality time or grand gestures crept into our collective consciousness, and we began thinking that we could make up for these neglected connections with "family time" or paid time off for our employees. This skewed perspective often causes us to justify our misaligned priorities by allowing our time on and off-duty to be hyper-dominated by the current task or goal or latest problem to solve, and we think we can simply make the missed time up to those we care about later.

This lack of perspective causes us to focus nearly all of our time, effort, and energy on what we do at work for various reasons, two of which I'd like to address. First, we gain so much of our identity from our profession. The odds are during any social introduction, you center on your profession, your team, and your organization. Very few people mention their children, families, or social clubs in their initial introductions. Second, there is a REAL short-term consequence to neglecting our day job. Fail to meet key performance indicators today, and you could be fired or miss out on future opportunities tomorrow. Alternatively, we can neglect our spouses for years before they have had enough and move on, or worse, find someone else.

We can often unintentionally neglect our children through thousands of micro-interactions each year that demonstrate they are less important to us than other things in our lives. Whether we are distracted while they show us their latest artwork from school, uninterested when they tell us a story, or are wrapping up a phone call from work as we walk in the door, we can constantly send the signal that they are not as important to us as whatever currently holds our attention.

Most people, even children, will eventually catch on and see the pattern for what it is, and as everyone wants to be heard and valued, they will inevitably go out and associate with people who demonstrate their interest and care better than we do. Teenage rebellion is often the result of unmet expectations and disappointment in not being heard and consistently valued by one's parents in tangible ways rather than a normal and inevitable byproduct of growing up.

The impacts of misplaced priorities are not confined to our households either. By focusing solely on the products of hard work, such as key performance indicators (KPI's), deadlines, and budgets, and neglecting the people part of the equation, we create a culture of disengaged, transactionally minded, and thereby transient employees who are with us only until better opportunities or better paychecks find them.

Worse, by not equipping ourselves and those we lead with practical tools to care for people, we can miss out on opportunities to catch negative mental health indicators early, when they are most treatable.

While not all of us have degrees in psychology and human behavior, each of us has a part to play in the well-being of those we're entrusted with leading. We have a role to play in their mental health and long-term character development, and the rewards for getting it right as a culture are healthy, high-performing team members that top the charts in both loyalty and engagement!

For those struggling to prioritize relationships and caring for people in this crazy digital world, the most important takeaway right now is that you are not facing this problem alone. Millions, if not billions, of people across the planet are struggling to work these problems out! Because you are not facing these problems alone, you don't have to solve them alone. It is time to bring these conversations to the forefront and collectively LEVEL UP!

For those that find it easy to prioritize relationships and are looking for ways to pass their skills on to help others, thank you! Growing healthy people is one of the highest callings in this life, and I believe that the tools in this book offer the proper framework for putting words to foundational human principles. Beyond that, they are the key to successfully repeating the process and teaching others to do precisely the same.

In this day and age, it is not enough to focus on workplace performance and expect that we will forge high-performing teams with solid retention where people LOVE coming to work every single day. The highest-performing teams put the development of their people at the forefront of their strategy, and the evidence says that it pays off!

So, if you are in the trenches and struggling every day, I hope this book is a guide to a healthier future for you, your family, and those you lead. Despite the ups and downs we all encounter, today marks the beginning of an upward trend in the relationships of those you hold most dear!

If you're re-reading this book and you are already in a healthy place, trending up, congratulations. Never let your guard down, as the world is always looking to suck you into new and competing priorities. I pray that this book helps you be more intentional about passing on what you've learned!

CHAPTER 2

We All Need Something Special

Van Halen's "Jump" blared through Kevin's earbuds in rhythm to his running stride. He wasn't in particularly great shape, but he had taken up running recently partly because his doctor had recommended more cardio in his routine and partly because it gave him an excuse to be alone and think.

Last night's dreams, the fight with his family, and his failure to meet his obligation were all fighting to overwhelm him. Through labored breaths he thought, *What's the solution? How can today be different? What are you going to do if she leaves you?*

He wrestled with himself for answers. *Stop making promises you can't keep. Stop making excuses. Own your stuff, Kevin...If she leaves you, you are going to die.* Those, and even more answers, went back and forth in his mind. Regardless of how reasonable these thoughts were, they competed with, *This isn't your fault. They're unreasonable. This will all pass, just give it time.*

By the time he made it back to the house, he was no closer to sorting out how he felt and what he should do than when he had started and therefore no more ready to face his family. He looked down at the keys in his hand and then at the front door before jumping in the car and putting the top down. After all, he had made a promise to get the order in that day, and maybe knocking that out first thing in the morning would do something to smooth things over.

About ten minutes later, he was sitting in the parking lot of Allyce's Garden Supplies, their local garden center, waiting for them to open. He was reviewing the list of supplies for Anthony's community project and bouncing between being frustrated with how things had played out and terrified at the prospect of finally pushing his wife over the edge and possibly losing her forever.

Once the store opened, he exited the car on autopilot. He had his list in his pocket and easily could have approached the first employee he saw but instead started meandering the aisles with no real destination in mind. Eventually, he found himself near the rear of the property where the more massive fruit trees and palms grew in oversized pots. Reaching out, his hand grazed several plants. He turned the leaves in his hands and lifted some to his nose while breathing in the sweet, earthy smell and taking in the profound simplicity.

He was so completely lost in his head, mindlessly walking the aisles, that he never saw the older gentleman who abruptly turned down his aisle and slammed into him. Kevin bounced back a few steps, but the man who bounced into him nearly lost his balance completely.

"Sorry I, uh, wasn't watching where I was going," Kevin said in embarrassment, rushing to the man's side.

He reached a hand out to help steady the stranger and was surprised to be greeted with a firm handshake and an ironlike grip.

A bit bewildered, Kevin returned the shake and got a good look at him for the first time. Appearing to be in his late 70's and built surprisingly strong for his wiry, aging frame, the man was dressed in a worn pair of Allyce's Garden Supplies employee overalls. He had kind eyes that seemed to take in all of the world's details and return an equal amount of wisdom.

His face held lines etched by long years of smiles and laughter and was accented by more than a bit of hardship and sadness.

"Are you ok?" Kevin asked.

The man patted himself down as if to feel for any broken bones and casually laughed, "Oh, it'll take worse than that to take me out, don't you worry. Now, where did I…"

He began looking around as if he had lost something. Spotting a pair of thin wire glasses, Kevin scooped them up and handed them over, noting the small pieces of tape holding them together in various places.

"Well, if you're sure you're ok, I'll leave you to it…"

"Now hold on," the elderly man said, stopping him. "Where were you off to in such a hurry?"

Kevin was unsure how to answer considering he hadn't actually been moving.

He stammered, "Well, I was, honestly…I was just walking. I've got a lot on my mind, and I truly didn't see you coming."

"Hmmm," the older man replied. "Walking around with a lot on your mind and no idea where you're going sounds like a dangerous way to go through life. Name's Frank."

He extended his hand for a proper shake this time.

Kevin extended his hand in return. "Kevin. Nice to meet you, Frank."

A few moments of silence passed between them before Kevin started to feel the need to fill it.

"It's beautiful out here," Kevin said, eyeing the rows of flowers, fruit trees, berry bushes, and hanging plants that seemed to continue as far as he could see. "Must be a lot of work keeping all these plants alive."

Frank gave a slight chuckle. "You'd think so, wouldn't you? That's not the case, though. Pretty easy to keep everything good and healthy once you know how."

"Maybe when you work here, but personally, I've never had much of a green thumb," Kevin said skeptically.

At this, Frank's demeanor changed, and he laughed joyfully, leaving Kevin wondering if he had missed the joke.

The Leader's Garden

"Green thumb, indeed. Nonsense, just suppose I had one nickel for every time someone said that, I swear they'd be paying for my funeral in nickels. Listen to me, son. Plants aren't complicated. In fact, plants are just like people; they need three simple things to thrive."

Frank reached for a small potted flower, holding it up for both of them to study.

"I'll give you that plants are easier to care for since they only need good soil, water, and sunlight, which are easy enough to find and in pretty good supply. Now, obviously, just like people, they all need different combinations of these things, but once you have the right mix," he paused, turning the plant before putting it back down again, "you just have to consistently stick to the formula."

Kevin barely noticed that Frank had paused for several seconds, only realizing it after catching Frank's unwavering eye contact.

"Take that cactus over there. It's not picky and certainly doesn't put up much of a fuss. Her needs are little, just some light, but she'll grow in the sun or the shade. She'll thrive in just about any soil, and we all know how far a little water goes with her."

Kevin wasn't sure what Frank was getting at, but he was utterly captivated. Not only was Frank's voice melodic and wise, but he spoke as one who had authority. More than that, Frank was sure of himself. Indeed, he seemed more confident than Kevin had been about anything in his life. Kevin had wholly forgotten why he had come here and was only concerned with giving Frank his full attention.

"Follow me over here," Frank said, walking towards a pond near the center of the property and beckoning Kevin to follow but not waiting for him.

As they approached one of the ponds, Frank stopped. "You see those water lilies there? Now compare them to our friend the cactus. On the surface, the two of them couldn't be more different, but believe it or not, they still have a lot in

The Leader's Garden

common. Wanna guess what that might be?"

Kevin wasn't sure he understood the question, but he gave it a shot, throwing out the first thing that came to mind. "They're both green?"

Frank laughed. "Come on now, have you been listening? You can do better than that. They both need the same things to thrive. What are they?"

Kevin's lightbulb went on. "Soil, sunshine, and water?"

"You got it!" Frank said excitedly. "Keeping plants healthy, even healing sick ones, is more about knowing the right combination of sunlight, soil, and water than about green thumbs and plant magic. You understand?"

Kevin nodded. "I think so."

"Good...Good. Now, why are you here? What can I do for you?"

Kevin took a minute to put his thoughts together, but eventually, he got out his list and explained everything Anthony needed for the Scout project's retaining wall. Frank wrote everything down in great detail and guaranteed everything would be delivered on time. Kevin let out a grateful sigh of relief. After working out the delivery details, Frank walked Kevin to the cashier and had him all checked out before the two said their goodbyes. Truthfully, though, Kevin had no desire to leave; he felt like he was barely scratching the surface of Frank's wisdom and just wished that Anthony had been here to meet him.

"Thanks for all of your help, Frank. It was really nice to meet you."

He didn't want to leave and honestly didn't know what else to say. After thanking Frank again, he headed back to the parking lot and was almost to his car when he heard Frank's voice calling after him.

"Kevin, hold on one minute!" Frank was walking briskly towards him. "Hold on now, son. Earlier, I forgot to tell you the most important part, the secret ingredient, the thing that holds it all together."

Kevin couldn't have cared less about plants; he barely remembered the sunlight, soil, and water thing. He had listened to Frank talk because of Frank. Still, he found himself hanging onto every word, spellbound by this older man with dirty brown hands who was wearing a pair of glasses older than he was.

With an almost mystical voice, Frank spoke. "It's consistency, Kevin. Consistency is the key. It's the difference between the hurt and the healthy, the growing and the dying. Consistency is where the real magic is. You remember that, and everything will turn out alright for you in the end, I promise you."

Kevin smiled a half-confused, half-grateful smile. Struggling to understand what he was feeling, he said, "Thank you again, Frank. I don't know why we met, but honestly, I feel like this was just what I needed today. I'll come back and visit again soon, I promise."

Kevin mentally poked himself for that last comment. Why was he promising to come back and visit some gardener he had just met when he could barely juggle his responsibilities as it was?

Kevin did his best to get through the rest of the day, avoiding conflict with Anthony and Julie and having what resembled a normal family dinner. Though things were still tense, Kevin tried to engage his family, and with Julie appearing the coldest, he started with Anthony.

"How was your day, son?" Kevin asked, trying his best to ignore the coldness from Julie.

Anthony responded, his demeanor seemingly returned to normal, "Good. My day was fine. I talked to our deacon, Mr. Justice, and let him know that everything was on track and would be delivered on time, so we are full steam ahead. How about you?"

Kevin was glad that Anthony seemed to be moving past yesterday and him running late with the order. His ability to get everything delivered on time was all that really mattered in the end, just as he had hoped.

Kevin tried bringing Julie into the conversation, hoping that she could move past this incident too. "Good. I didn't tell you guys, but I had the strangest encounter this morning at the garden center with an older gentleman. Frank was his name, I think. For some reason, he was giving me a botany lesson, taking me all over the property before I was finally able to break away." He paused, taking a bite of his dinner. "Really nice old man, though. It's too bad you didn't meet him…"

Julie stood up and said, "Thank you for the nice dinner conversation. I'm going to bed," before she walked away.

Kevin and Anthony sat in silence for a few moments before Kevin sighed, stood up, and headed into the kitchen. Anthony cleared the table while Kevin started washing the dishes without another word being spoken between them. When they finished, they went their separate ways, and eventually Kevin found himself in bed with the lights off, staring at the empty ceiling.

He was replaying his conversation with Frank in his head over and over again. He turned the words over in his mind, trying to figure out why the moment had moved him so deeply. It was just a passing encounter, one that should have been easily forgotten, but that just wasn't the case. Kevin felt like he had missed something important. *Was there something between the lines, something in Frank's words that was unsaid?*

One particular phrase kept coming back to the surface, and Kevin just couldn't stop replaying it.

Plants are just like people; they all need three things to thrive.
Plants are just like people; they all need three things to thrive.
Plants are just like people; they all need three things to thrive.

Internally, Kevin was practically screaming at himself. *How are plants like people? What three things do people need to thrive?* It was nearly midnight. He should have been asleep, but at that moment, he wanted nothing more in the world than the answer to that question.

What do people need to thrive? Kevin couldn't quite place his finger on why, but internally, he had this irrational feeling that he had missed something profound, as if the holy grail had been offered to him and he hadn't recognized it for what it was. Without truly understanding why, Kevin committed to action and made a promise to himself. Tomorrow, he would go back to the garden center and learn whatever secrets Frank had left to tell him. The decision brought a peace to Kevin, and he had the first good night's sleep he had had in months.

===========The Big Idea===========

Like plants, people need intentional care to thrive and produce good fruit. When we calibrate our care to each individual plant's needs, it becomes more resilient and can weather greater hardship all while producing more prominent, bountiful fruit.

The inverse is also true, sadly. Not having a green thumb with both plants and people is often simply the result of failing to understand your charge properly and neglecting to provide for their specific needs in the right way at the right time.

Understanding what people need and their specific "formula" for thriving is an interpersonal hack that is both practical and actionable. It allows us to identify the root issues we are dealing with and create a concrete plan of action, which when implemented consistently will drive change in the lives of those we lead!

===========Exercise===========

Take a minute and think of the people you feel most responsible for both at home and at work, and answer the following questions:

1. Who are the happiest, healthiest, and bearing the most fruit?
2. Who are the people that are struggling the most professionally or relationally?
3. Of all those listed, who would thrive most with more intentionality on your part?

CHAPTER 2
Reflection

"Do unto others as you would have them do unto you." Luke 6:31

To me, "doing unto others as you would have them do unto you" is an important part of being a strong leader. Considering how many people have tackled the idea of "doing unto others" in the past, I find this reflection challenging to write because I feel a colossal duty to bring something new to light.

Throughout my career, I have heard two predominantly different takes on the Golden Rule from Luke 6:31 as it relates to leadership. I can sum them up as:
1. Be the leader you wish you had when you were in their position.
2. Treat other people the way you wish you would have been treated.

While I am a firm believer in the Golden Rule as it is written in the Bible, I believe that both of these interpretations miss the mark almost entirely.

If you are one of the great human beings out there trying to be the leader you wish you had, unfortunately, I have some bad news for you. First, your memory of the past is flawed in regard to both the situation you were in and the person you were at the time. While there is value in understanding your past and using it to refine current patterns of behavior, there are drawbacks when applying it to the way you treat others. The past is never quite what we remember it as being, and because we are talking about lived experience, we are both biased and blind to a great deal of what was going on in all past situations. Therefore, simply trying to lead people the way you wish you had been led when you were younger is unlikely to be the cure-all for the situations that you find yourself in today.

Second, and likely far more critical, is that you are not, will not, and cannot ever lead a carbon copy of you! By the time I was in my late 20's, I had lost several friends to drug overdose and suicides, had run-ins with the police, and had almost been kicked out of the Air Force. I needed a particular leadership style and an incredibly determined leader to see me through that. I brought abandonment issues, mental health issues, and several suitcases of baggage to the table. The odds of today's me ever encountering past me and successfully leading me well are virtually zero. Endeavoring to be the leader I wish I would have had back then practically ensures I won't be the leader my people need me to be RIGHT NOW. The people I am leading today are not carbon copies of past me; instead, they are unique human beings who carry their own baggage and have hearts filled with their own wants, goals, dreams, and desires.

Trying to influence the lives of others by being anything other than the leader THEY need today based on their personality and situation they find themselves in will likely only stunt their growth at best and prevent them from reaching their true potential at worst.

As for the second interpretation, "treating other people the way you want to be treated," I will first speak to its merits. Regarding basic human dignity, you must ingrain this rule into your thoughts, actions, and behavior patterns everywhere you have influence. I believe that we all want leaders who treat us with dignity and respect. We all want to be heard, valued and appreciated, and seen for who we are.

In this regard, the Golden Rule as written is a grand slam.

I believe there is another, better interpretation of the Golden Rule as it applies to leadership, however, and it is this: Be the leader the other person needs you to be right now.

I realize that this idea seems simplistic and self-evident on its face, but let's break down the idea. If we are going to be the leaders our people need us to be, the prerequisite is that we know what type of leadership they need. The type of leadership they need is based on many factors, but the two largest in my mind are their personality and the situation they are going through.

For starters, our internal wiring and the individual aspects of our personalities and worldviews govern much of what motivates us, what inspires us, what causes us stress, and what brings us joy. Personality assessments are great interpersonal accelerators that can help us get to know both ourselves and others better. That's why I am such a vocal advocate for 5 Voices, which is the best personality profile program I have ever experienced. You can take the online assessment and get your free personality report at http://voices.marktilsher.com.

Endeavoring to understand the tendencies, strengths, weaknesses, experiences, and trials of those we lead is so crucial to leading them well. Only by combining our understanding of those we lead with an understanding of the journey they are on can we ever truly become leaders of influence in their lives and help them steer through the countless challenges they will no doubt face.

The metaphor of the leader's garden comes into play here, as learning that plants need soil, sunlight, and water is easy, but understanding how to make each individual species thrive and bear good fruit is a lifelong endeavor. There is no gardener on the planet that has the perfect gardening style, since there is no style that would be perfect for every plant. Indeed, any gardener that tried to force their garden to adapt to their pet peeves, strengths, and weaknesses would soon find themselves out of a job.

I believe that attempting to force those we lead into adapting to our style of leadership is where most of us get this wrong and by a large margin. For example, you will undoubtedly lead people who need clear guidelines, defined milestones, and regular check-ins. Conversely, you will have people that will feel stifled unless they have wide lanes, clear objectives, and lots of physical and mental space to work.

There will be people on your teams that rarely take anything personally and seek critical feedback to refine their ideas. I would also expect to find people on your teams that find it difficult to separate themselves from their work or their ideas and find critical feedback harsh and react emotionally to it. In all of these cases, choosing to go all in on your default gear will be life-giving to one group while soul-crushing to the other. Leading people the way they need to be led means growing our influence without resorting to our default gear or insisting that everyone around us adapt to our leadership styles.

Believing that your leadership style is supreme or that by adapting to you everyone will thrive is the ultimate hubris and the source of virtually every toxic leadership story I encounter. Inevitably, when you refuse to adapt your leadership practice to those you lead and instead force those you lead to adapt to you, only those that adapt to you best will thrive, which often causes the perception of favoritism and even "the good ol' boy system."

Because there is no one-size-fits-all approach to growing healthy, high-performing people, you cannot allow anyone on your team to function as if their style is "the one." Instead, our subleaders must be trained, educated, and mentored into viewing their subordinates as individuals that require a unique calibration of things like communication, structure, motivation, and yes, even discipline.

While committing to changing our own patterns is one thing, mentoring our subleaders into this new way of thinking is an entirely different challenge. When someone is causing the types of issues we've been discussing and continues leaning into their pride and demonstrating arrogance in leadership, there is little we can do to help them in the short term. I believe, and I don't say this lightly, the best use of your time can sometimes be in finding their replacement, as changing their mind and humbling them is often a long, grueling process, not for the faint of heart.

As to the second part, "right now," it is critical that we know three pieces of information before we endeavor to lead anyone. Where is the person now, how much time do you have together, and how far can you reasonably expect the person to grow in that time? Without considering these three questions, you are following your gut, steering with your emotions, or throwing darts in the dark.

Therefore, I urge you to consider those you are charged with and make lists of their best and worst tendencies. Next, ask yourself: What are the consequences if each tendency, positive or negative, is allowed to dominate? Now look at where you see each tendency playing out at work/home depending on the relationship. Finally, consider what you can reasonably do to help them see their tendency, focus on nurturing the positive, and begin to prune the negative.

In summary, if we are going to lead people and lead them well, we have to have a deep understanding of who they are and what they are going through. Only then can we adapt our strategy and our tactics to the current developmental objective and internal and external stressors. In my opinion, that is the essence of the Golden Rule of leadership. Committing to the lifelong endeavor of knowing our people and what they are going through is the foundational principle that the rest of this book is built upon.

Without an individualized approach, we will forever be limited to influence only the people that respond best to our default leadership style. Moving past this limiting mindset is foundational to becoming a leader worth following and a true gardener of healthy people!

CHAPTER 3

What Are You Fighting For?

Kevin practically raced to the garden center the next morning and once again found himself sitting in the car, not sure if he was even going to go in. Last night had been tense with his family but not outright explosive, and the last thing he remembered was promising himself he would head straight here when they opened. Kevin had promised Frank that he would come back, and he was trying to knock his promises off the list where he could. Besides, he had gone to bed feeling seriously curious about what he had missed with the old man yesterday.

This morning, however, the feelings were slightly different. Sure, he was still curious, but now he felt pretty foolish about the whole thing. *Why did I even come back here? Do I really think some random gardener is going to have the secrets to solving all of my problems?*

For a minute, he considered putting the car in reverse and driving himself back home. He imagined a thousand reasons he was about to make a fool of himself. What if he had misunderstood Frank yesterday? What if the gardener had nothing but platitudes to offer, the ramblings of an old man and nothing more? Wrestling with the desperation he felt, he eventually decided to follow through and talk with Frank one more time if for no other reason than to close out his promise to come back and to prove to himself that things were beyond repair and past the point of no return.

With the decision behind him, Kevin allowed a small amount of hope to creep into the edges of his consciousness. What if Frank had something valuable to give him? What if there was something he was missing? With resignation but also a bit of excitement, he walked into the garden center's main building to find Frank.

Before he even laid eyes on Frank, the old man's familiar voice called out to him.

"Kevin! Son, is that you? Back already? You forget something yesterday? I'm afraid it might be too late to add to your order!"

Kevin felt relief rush over him. Something about Frank put him immediately at ease and almost made him feel foolish for all of the self-doubt and trepidation. Why had he worked himself up over the visit? Being back in the man's presence, Kevin felt like a student again. He started to talk, to explain he had just come back to talk, but Frank rushed past that.

"Day's calling. Got things to do. Got to make it count. Not sure how many I've got left, after all."

Frank produced a handkerchief and wiped sweat from his forehead, then motioned for Kevin to walk with him while he worked. The two quickly picked up conversation like a couple of old friends. As they talked, Frank invited him into his past, pointing out his daughter's favorite flower over here, and over there, the plant his wife had given him on their anniversary years ago. Time passed slowly while they walked, and once again, Kevin almost forgot why he had come at all.

As the conversation hit a natural lull, the silence began to hang in the air, only the rhythmic thump of sprinklers and steady pace of voices around them fighting off any awkwardness. Frank seemed disinclined to break the silence. He eyed Kevin for several seconds.

As soon as Kevin glanced Frank's way, Frank said, "Well, out with it already."

Kevin didn't immediately understand what Frank was asking, so he grasped for a response but came up empty, and Frank added patiently, "What brought you here today?"

Kevin, more than a little flustered, stopped walking. "What? Oh. Well…It's just…" He took a breath. "Ok. I am sure this is silly. I don't even know where to start, but here goes. Yesterday, when we were talking, you said something. You said that people needed three things to thrive, just like plants."

Frank maintained an attentive posture and nodded in affirmation, encouraging Kevin to keep talking.

"Right now, it feels like my life is falling apart, and I don't know exactly why, but something called me back here. I'm sorry I didn't ask yesterday, but honestly, I almost missed it. I guess I was hoping you'd be willing to finish the thought, then I'll leave and you never have to be bothered by me again. That's not foolish, is it?"

"No, not foolish at all. Not bringing coffee with you when asking for advice though, now that might be foolish," he said with a smile. "Let me think." He was obviously holding back with Kevin as he seemed to try and remember their conversation. "I say a lot of things. Hard to keep them straight sometimes. I said plants were like people. You're sure that was it?"

Usually, Kevin would have taken the good-natured playfulness for what it was, even returned it in kind, but Kevin was already on the edge of walking away, and he seemed to be getting all the confirmation he needed that he was on a fool's errand. Still, he was compelled by something he didn't understand—to hear what Frank had alluded to in yesterday's conversation, and so he tried one more time.

He responded with measured patience. "I'm sure that was it. You said plants were like people in that both needed three things to thrive, or something close to that."

Frank's eyes twinkled. "Hmm. I seem to remember something like that now that you mention it. Humor me for a minute though, young man. *Why?*" He paused, letting the last word hang in the air with a gravity that emphasized the question's importance. "Why do you want to know?"

The question stopped Kevin in his tracks, so much so that Frank took a moment to notice and turn back towards him. *Why does he want to know? Is that a rhetorical question? Surely everyone wants to know the answer to that question. What justification is Frank looking for?*

"I don't...I'm not sure how to answer that," Kevin said flatly. "What do you want me to say?"

"Oh, sure you do," Frank chided him. "What is this all about? Why do you care?"

The question forced Kevin to reflect. He had been hiding the truth from himself, burying it under resentment and frustration, but deep down, he knew why he cared. He was terrified, his marriage was near its breaking point, and he wasn't sure if there were weeks or even days left before it expired. His relationship with his son felt like it was pulled tight enough to snap. Kevin just wanted everything to go back to the way it used to be, for someone or something to quell the storm.

"Well, out with it," Frank poked.

"Why do I want to know? Well..." The dam broke, and the first emotion to pour out was fear. "I have problems. My son and I are barely on speaking terms. My wife and I, we fight more than we talk, and I am absolutely drowning in people's problems at work. Every day, I bounce from one thing to the next, and I don't even know where I am going anymore. I don't know what to do anymore...I need help, Frank." He paused, surprised at just how much was pent up inside of him, then he barely whispered, "I just need help."

Kevin continued, "I'm afraid, Frank. What if I lose them? Worse, what if I can never make them happy or be the leader they need me to be? What if it's all gotten too messy to fix?"

His voice trailed off on the last sentence. Kevin was tapping into something he didn't fully understand yet.

As the fear ran its course, another primal emotion began to show itself: anger. "No one seems to get how hard it all is to keep together. I work twelve- to sixteen-hour days sometimes just to keep things moving, and when I do drop a ball, there is no grace...no mercy. My son barely acknowledges our authority these days, and the trouble I'm having at work is undeserved and unnecessary. It shouldn't be this hard, Frank. It just shouldn't be this hard."

The words settled between the two men, while Kevin, too embarrassed to look up, kept his eyes on the ground.

When Kevin spoke again, he was emotionally exhausted. "I don't know why I came back here, Frank. I don't know you. You don't know me, but for some reason, something inside of me says you have answers, and if you can help me, I'm ready to listen."

Kevin, finally getting it all out, was rocked when he looked up at the old man's face. He wasn't sure exactly what he had expected, but undoubtedly, it was something like empathy, sympathy, or even pity. Instead, he met eyes unmoved by his outburst.

"Humph," Frank exhaled. "I was afraid of that. Life's gotten harder than it should be. Well, who said it was supposed to be easy, hmm? I can sum up the bulk of human history in about three words: life is hard. Relationships aren't built around nice buildings and air conditioning. They take hard, intentional, daily work. Now, this is more important than you can imagine, son, so I'm going to ask you the question again, and this time I want a clear answer out of you, so I'm going to give you a clearer question."

Frank suddenly felt twenty years younger.

He locked eyes with Kevin and questioned him with the authority of a prophet. "Do you want to know what I have to say to make your life better, or are you here because you want to make THEIR lives better? Are you here because you're desperate, Kevin, or are you here because you want to FIGHT?

Do you want to fight for your son because you want the best for him, or do you want to fight for him because you're tired of fighting with him? And as far as your work problems, these problems got a name?"

Kevin, stunned, barely muttered, "Eric."

"Eric, eh? Well, my guess is you want to fix things with Eric because it would take more work to FIRE Eric. Is that it, or are you here because you have HIS best in mind? Those are the questions I want to know the answer to." Frank continued. "So what is it? Who is this all about? Who's the real problem here?"

Kevin had no words. He locked gazes with the old gardener, his eyes burning with magma and his breath coming in small strained puffs. Kevin's pride dominated his thoughts, and he wanted nothing more in that moment than to put this simpleton in his place. How dare he question his commitment to his employees, or worse, his love for his wife and child!

He felt like an absolute fool for believing he was going to learn anything here. Kevin hadn't come back to be insulted. He had exposed himself, made himself vulnerable, only to have his motives and character put on trial. Kevin couldn't understand the true source of his rage, not at that moment. His pride was a dam, thick and well-built, holding back the progress he was desperate for.

"This was a mistake," Kevin said quietly. "I shouldn't have come back." He paused, then said, "Thank you for helping with my son's project, Frank. I'll make sure he knows what you did for us."

With that, he turned abruptly on his heels and left. Frank made no effort to stop him.

Less than a minute later, Kevin was on the road, taking the long route home. *Who does he think he is? How dare he attack me like that. I have never done anything but LOVE my family, and I'm supposed to listen to him? To take advice from him?*

It was almost an hour later when Kevin realized that his phone had been buzzing, and he had missed more than one text from his wife. He had promised they would hit the farmers

market and spend the day together, and he was late again.
.

===========The Big Idea===========

All of the emotional intelligence in the world won't help you grow healthy people if your motives are based in self-interest or self-preservation. When doing things for our own benefit or if our primary motivations are performance, convenience, or glory, at best, we make people feel like valuable tools. At worst, they feel undervalued and even manipulated. Learning to orient yourself to be FOR others and not for yourself is the greatest leadership lesson I have ever learned, and I fight to achieve it every day.

===========Exercise===========

Make a list of your immediate family and team, and ask yourself the following for each person:

1. Do I truly want the best for them, regardless of how it benefits me/the team?
2. AM I completely FOR THEM and ready to fight for their best no matter our relationship status or circumstances?
3. If the answer to either question is no, write a single sentence summarizing why.

CHAPTER 3
Reflection

"Most of us are experts at solving other people's problems, but we generally solve them in terms of our own and the advice we give is seldom for other people but for ourselves." Nan Fairbrother

Being entrusted to lead other human beings and influence their lives is one of life's greatest joys. Unfortunately, that joy comes with a tremendous amount of responsibility and no small number of frustrations attached. Those who answer the call and meet these challenges head-on leave a lasting legacy.

If you are anything like me, you often find yourself supersaturated in tasks, overworked, and buried under a self-replicating to-do list. To make matters worse, if you are anything like me, human beings tend to get on our nerves. People tend to push our buttons, to disappoint us, and to fall short of virtually every standard we can set for them. To emphasize this point, we don't have to look any further than the highway. I have personally driven all across the United States, the Middle East, Europe, and Korea. In all of my travels, the only commonality I have found is that people universally seem to feel that anyone driving faster than them is unsafe and anyone going slower is a moron.

The point is simply this: We often have a tendency to become consumed with what WE want, where WE want to go, and the problems WE face around us. When we focus on our wants, goals, needs, ambitions, and problems, lumping people into the problem category and viewing them as obstacles to overcome is far too easy.

Putting people into the problem category isn't always without merit, to our credit. I have had countless interactions with people who were less than kind, caring, and even competent, and I mean in my organizations, on my team, and even in my family.

The hard truth is that even when people are less than kind, caring, and, yes, even competent, our interactions with them are always an opportunity for growth, both ours and theirs, even when the people themselves feel like the problem. Our challenge therefore, even in the midst of our frustration, is to determine what type of opportunity is presenting itself. We must be continually asking ourselves the following questions:

1. What is the opportunity here for my personal growth?
2. What opportunity is here for their personal growth?
3. Is it reasonable to think that I can help them grow through this?

When it comes to our personal growth, committing to understanding the root cause of our behaviors and implementing goals to change our patterns are great first steps. When it comes to their personal growth, we have to be sure that our interactions with others are based on a reasonable expectation that we can help develop them. On top of that, when attempting to develop others, we must be absolutely sure that our intent is less about transferring our negative emotions to them and more about bringing out the best in them.

The call here is to commit to always hunting for growth opportunities, even when the world gives us every reason imaginable to fight WITH people rather than for them. Sadly, too few people realize that developing and growing others is where the true path to influence and a lasting legacy is found.

If you have trouble visualizing what I mean, think back to every leader who has positively impacted you. In most cases, the most common people that come to mind are coaches, teachers, supervisors, or family members. Regardless of who comes to mind during this exercise, I guarantee that one commonality rings true for every reader of this book: The person you are thinking of wanted the absolute best for you and was willing to push, even fight, to unlock your potential and make the best version of you a reality.

Over twenty years ago, a young Air Force staff sergeant named Kevin Chronister impacted my life in a way that caused me to commit my life to fighting for the best in others. The impact he had on my life was so powerful that, to this day, I tell parts of the story every time I speak on stage. With this book, I am challenging you to have that same level of influence in the lives of those you lead, which can only happen when you are overwhelmingly for them and committed to their absolute best.

Fighting for the best in others is a choice that, if we are faithful to it, has the potential to realign the way we think, feel, and act. Finally, committing to this realignment will con challenge you to be and do better daily and for the rest of your life.

Imagine a world where leaders fought hardest FOR people they lead rather than their own wants, needs, and ambitions, as is all too often the case. Leaders that are committed to self-awareness and personal growth are desperately needed, and they are one of the key predictors of team performance.

Never forget that everyone around you is either going through something traumatic or is in between traumatic experiences. Everyone you know, in all circles of influence, will lose people close to them. They will all deal with tragic diseases in themselves or the people they love. They will have accidents, rack up crippling debt, or find themselves caring for a relative they are ill-equipped to handle. For the lucky few of us not dealing with some tragedy in our lives, we are often supporting our friends and loved ones who are.

I know that is a turn toward the dark side. Still, the main point I am trying to make is that the people around you are likely going through something you are oblivious to. Regardless of what you know about their situations, you can sometimes have a significant impact on how much their struggles impact their mental, physical, and spiritual health. Never underestimate the power of one champion. One truly passionately compassionate leader, friend, family member, or mentor can be the difference between life and death.

To emphasize that point, when speaking, I find myself returning to stories of suicidal bridge jumpers whose plans changed when someone cared enough to step in. The internet is full of stories of people seconds away from ending their lives who ended up having an extraordinary impact on our world simply because one person took time to stop and quite literally talk them off of the ledge.

In one remarkable real-life story "She almost jumped off a bridge. She now returns there to post notes that have saved the lives of others." written by Sydney Page from the Washington Post, is about a fantastic human, Paige Hunter, who was once seconds from jumping from the Wearmouth Bridge. Paige, who nearly plunged to her death, was saved when two passersby stopped to tell her just how valuable she truly was. That moment changed Paige's entire perspective; she now devotes her life to paying that blessing forward. Paige spends countless hours every month posting hand-written inspirational notes on bridges and across town, encouraging others not to give up. To this day, Paige continues to receive messages from people who were ready to commit suicide but turned from that path by finding one of Paige's notes. Many of them have been so inspired, they have taken to writing notes of their own and posting them all over town.

Never underestimate the power one person can have on the life of another human being and, ultimately, the entire world. You have the power to save someone's life by simply being attentive and responsive to their needs! Perhaps that statement seems a bit overwhelming or farfetched. Maybe you cannot imagine yourself as a person of influence. The good news is you can grow your influence and impact on people; the bad news is that it doesn't happen overnight and it isn't easy. Indeed, it is a skill that must be learned like any other, and it takes time, dedication, and more than a bit of focus to master. Also, just when you think you have this down, you will often be entrusted to lead someone that puts everything you have learned and come to rely on to the test. For now, however, let's lock down where to start.

The first step towards influence and true impact is becoming intentional about what we are aiming for. Setting your goals is so critical because what you aim for ultimately governs what you see. For example, if you aim for justice, you see injustice in the world around you. If you aim for entrepreneurship, everywhere you look you see opportunity! Never forget that making a decision and committing to it is integral to putting your subconscious to work for you!

If your goal is to grow healthy, high-performing people, then it must be done through influence, and the first step is to start focusing on the best in the lives of those you lead and prioritizing their development by hunting for growth opportunities. Once you commit to this foundational principle, then, like magic, opportunities to develop the people you lead will begin to appear around every corner.

CHAPTER 4

Something Has to Change

"Eric, what do you expect me to do? You didn't show up to the site yesterday. I was counting on you. And good on your team, but damn it, Eric, they covered for you, and not for the first time. We're all stuck picking up your slack because you're not there to do your job!"

Kevin was at the tail end of his anger and started to slip back into tense frustration. He liked Eric, had high hopes for him, and sincerely just wanted things to go back to the way they were. Why had everything gotten so difficult?

When he spoke again, there was disappointment in his voice, but the anger was bleeding out. For his part, Eric stayed silent with his head down.

"I expect more out of you, Eric." Kevin continued, "What is going on with you? You know I respect you. We all do, but we can't have this conversation again. I need your best, and so does your team. We all expect better from you. You deserve better from yourself."

Kevin stared at Eric, who still hung his head, seemingly in shame. Kevin noted how defeated Eric looked. He seemed lost, distracted, unable to focus, almost somewhere else. Although the last thing Kevin wanted was to let Eric go, he was starting to think their relationship was just another one beyond repair, ready to be tossed onto the pile with the others.

"Well? What do you have to say?" Kevin chided.

Though Kevin and Eric weren't friends, Kevin had trusted him and respected him deeply. He had grown to depend on Eric, and the recent slip in performance and lack of communication only compounded the betrayal he was feeling. Still, it wasn't like Kevin to blow up haphazardly, and in the moment, shame crept in at the way he had let loose. Before he could walk it back and apologize, Eric responded, catching him completely by surprise.

"Do you even care?" Eric's words, a massive fist, slammed into Kevin's chest, stealing the breath from his lungs and pushing him back on his heels mentally. Eric continued his assault with verbal jabs and hooks. "Have you ever asked me where I was, Kevin? What I was doing last week? Does it even matter?"

"I..." Kevin tried to counter but couldn't mount a defense.

The onslaught continued, one punch after another.

"All you talk about is YOUR expectations, Kevin. Your disappointment. Do you even care what's going on with me, or am I just another tool in your toolbox?"

Eric's voice blasted through Kevin's office door despite it being closed, ringing clearly throughout the halls and perking ears up across the office even if heads stayed down.

"Eric, lower your voice..." Kevin tried to insist, but there was no weight behind his words.

His verbal counter-punches were soft, and Eric brushed them off. Eric was leaning forward in his chair now.

Typically humble and reserved, he pushed his glasses farther up the bridge of his nose, then continued the verbal assault. "Lower my voice? You know what, Kevin? My team is kicking ass right now, even with me barely holding it together. Have I failed you? Have they? No. I haven't failed you, and I promise you I will die before I fail them. I thought that meant something to you. I guess I was wrong."

Kevin tried one last time to control the situation and protect himself, even if he couldn't mount a defense. He was desperate to buy time.

"Eric, I'm sorry..."

But Eric wasn't listening, he just kept at it. "If I am such a disappointment to you, BOSS, maybe you should just replace me with someone else. God knows I've turned down more than one job offer this month alone..."

Eric pushed himself to his feet and walked out of Kevin's office without another word, leaving the door open behind him.

Kevin called out, "Eric, wait..." but his words fell on deaf ears. Futilely, he tried one more time. "Eric, get back here..."

Eric had already left the building and was likely halfway to his car already.

What have I done? Kevin thought as he sat in his office poring over the conversation, and all he could think about was how badly he had erred.

Eric had been on Kevin's team for nearly two years and until now had given Kevin no reason to doubt him. Quite the opposite. Kevin had come to depend on the man's intelligence, work ethic, and drive to get the job done. In return for all he brought to the table, Eric was drawing a sizable salary and was leading the most technical team on Kevin's payroll. Two things Kevin had expected to earn: Eric's loyalty and (with everything hanging by a thread at home) lightening his own load. Now, not only was Kevin not making progress towards lightening his load and reducing his own stress, he may have just taken a huge leap backwards.

===

1:00 AM. Kevin gasped for air as he lurched up in bed. He froze, halfway between the real and the dream worlds. His senses gradually came around as his mind came to grips with what had woken him. Had he heard a noise? He looked over at his wife, Julie, sleeping peacefully next to him. Even at this hour, with moonlight barely making its way through the curtains, Kevin was overcome by just how beautiful she was and how little he deserved her. Though his head was foggy, as he stared at her, all he could do was regret that they had gone to bed angry again after fighting about him coming home late.

In an instant, Kevin was flooded with a flashback of the dream that had woken him flooded his senses. He remembered images of his parents sitting on the couch in front of him, his hands full of soaked tissue. How the dream had momentarily slipped past him, he couldn't understand.

"Kevin, we're sorry, son, but your father and I have to get this divorce. It's not you, honey..." his mom was saying softly.

Her voice, always soothing and comforting, was falling flat. He barely heard her above his sniffles.

"But...but...I'll be good, I promise. I'm sorry..." 8-year-old Kevin's voice was barely decipherable above his sobs. He reached a hand bursting with tissue up to his nose and blew.

His father took the opportunity to chime in. "Son, it isn't you. We love you. We both do. But sometimes, unfortunately, relationships can be too broken to fix. Sometimes there's just nothing you can do. Not every relationship can be saved..."

The words "sometimes there's nothing you can do" and "not every relationship can be saved" echoed in his mind over and over as if he were committing important principles to memory.

From that moment in his life, Kevin had watched important relationships around him fall apart. It had started with his parents but would envelop his extended family before long. His love life had been full of premature breakups, and he had far too many friendships that had expired before their due date. Kevin had, unconsciously, been carrying those words around like a cross his entire life. He threw in the towel when things got terrible and relationships got tough. While Kevin wasn't a quitter, when the relationships in his life became strained, he tended to view them as hopeless and move on. The main thing holding his marriage together, at least from his end, was that he had long ago made a promise to himself that he would never leave his family no matter how hard things got, no matter the cost.

Still, his father's words echoed in his head. "Sometimes there's nothing you can do…"

Kevin spoke softly to himself without realizing it, "You don't believe, that do you?"

He wasn't his father. He was never going to be his father.

Julie stirred beside him. Still asleep, she asked, "Are you ok?", before falling back asleep nearly instantly.

It wouldn't have mattered if he hadn't answered; she wouldn't have heard him anyway. Still, he whispered, "Everything's fine. Everything's going to be fine…"

Kevin wasn't sure what was going on in his head, why he was dreaming so vividly, but one thing was solidifying in his head: He was going to fight. He loved Julie and Anthony. He cared more about them than his own life, and if he had to lay it all down to make their marriage work, then so be it.

He lay in bed for the next hour, processing his racing thoughts before finally succumbing to sleep.

===========The Big Idea===========

Truly seeing ourselves through another's eyes can be an emotionally challenging experience but is often a prerequisite to real and lasting change. As long as we allow ourselves to become defensive, justify our actions, or return fire when it feels like punches are coming our way, we stunt our growth and limit our potential.

The hope is that these moments offer us a leadership mirror that we can gaze into and see ourselves and our actions for what they truly are. Engaging our families and teams proactively before the conflict comes and asking them for real, honest, and direct feedback on who we are and how we make them feel is a gateway to becoming the best version of ourselves. When it comes to soliciting feedback, a good rule of thumb is, the more often the better!

Obviously, asking for feedback can be a bit uncomfortable if you are not used to it, but I encourage you to lean into the process and aggressively refine your rough tendencies until they shine like diamonds or fade away altogether.

===========Exercise===========

Consider your key relationships (family, team, community, etc.), and commit to asking at least three people on your team/in your family the following questions:

1. What is one negative behavior I display that you think I should do less often or eliminate?
2. What is one positive behavior that I display that you think I should do more often?

3. Can you help me see any blind spots where I may damage relationships unintentionally?

CHAPTER 4
Reflection

"We do not learn from experience... we learn from reflecting on experience" John Dewey

Throughout my Air Force career, our leadership constantly reinforced the idea that we were the best of America's best. While I genuinely believe that to be true, I don't think America's best gravitate to the military. In all sincerity, I believe the exact opposite is true.

For the most part, I believe that the US military attracts many of our country's young people that are lost, forgotten, and even hopeless. Many who join the armed forces struggle to find their place in society before enlisting and honestly have nowhere else to go.

That being said, I do believe that the US military produces the best of America's best, and here is why: I believe that the military does exceptionally well at forcing us through a mold that shaves off our most abrasive parts and guides us through examining the baggage we had been carrying around to our detriment all our lives. This intentional stripping away of the outer layers gets at the person underneath. The military's approach is to tear down soldiers and then build them up. This process, while painful, is the same process you need to undergo if you are going to get to the heart of the misbeliefs that shape your behavior and impact the people around you that you care about most.

The process of understanding who you are and why you do what you do is a never-ending cycle, a perpetual roller coaster ride you should never disembark. At the end of the day, who you are, your tendencies, and your misbeliefs are yours to own, and just like our US service members, you have a choice to break down and rebuild the parts of you that you like the least.

Fortunately, or unfortunately for most of us, there is no dramatic life event like basic military training that forces us to re-examine all of our understandings and misconceptions about how we should orient ourselves to the world around us all at once. Instead, most of us learn through trial and error over a much longer time horizon. I encourage you to become obsessively proactive about understanding how your actions impact those around you to accelerate your growth and, consequently, your impact. Two foundational ways to do this are through self-reflection and through seeking feedback.

On the topic of self-reflection, consider the Harvard Business School study from 2014 titled "Making Experience Count: The Role of Reflection in Individual Learning." My takeaway from their study, was that simply taking time to reflect on experiences and training had a dramatic impact on both learning and performance, even eclipsing time spent on practicing the skills in question. So, what can we do with this information? Well, if you are in a position of authority, offer your people fifteen minutes at the end of each day to reflect, in silence, as a team! You may just improve your team's performance by up to 22%! For those of you not in a position of authority, start baking personal reflection time into your daily routine today!

In the context of this book and our work together, one way to accelerate our growth, improve our relationships, and influence those around us is to simply take fifteen minutes at the end of each day and set it aside for mental or hand-written reflection. Consider what went well and what didn't go well. Where did you make the biggest gains and see the biggest setbacks? Based on my understanding of the research, the act of reflection itself is where the power lies, not in the method!

Another way to improve our influence with others and understand the impact that we have on them is to consistently seek feedback on behavior patterns and strive to refine the negative and double down on the positive. Simply asking regularly what behaviors people think you should do more or less of is a great place to start!

One hurdle in our way is the tendency to get defensive when we are not solely responsible for the situation or both sides in a conflict bear part of the responsibility. If, as I have previously stated, every situation we encounter is an opportunity for self-reflection and growth, then we have to take action on our part of the problem, even if we are only 1% wrong to their 99%.

So, from now on, understand that no matter how damaged the relationships around you have become, no matter how dire your circumstances are, you are the one thing you can control. You are the one thing you can endeavor to change from the beginning of your life to the end.

Human history is full of broken people who have overcome insurmountable internal obstacles to become people worth following. Our tendencies and negative patterns do not have to define us. They can just be the beginning of your story of growth! Regardless of who you are and what you have been through, I believe you can have a tremendous impact.

You have in you the capacity to do AMAZING things, and I believe in you.

The Leader's Garden

CHAPTER 5

It's Time

Green Day blared through Kevin's earbuds as his feet carried him through his Saturday morning run. He had woken up, gotten out of bed, and raced out the door, once again before anyone else was even up. Kevin's mind was racing faster than his feet as he thought back to his explosion with Eric yesterday and the offense, he had taken with Frank's direct questioning the day before. Kevin couldn't ignore the connection, and honestly, he found that he didn't want to sidestep it. More, he wanted to hunt for the connection, the root cause that was driving him to be shorter and shorter with the people around him.

While his sleep last night had been dreamless, his brain seemed to have worked furiously, strategizing what his next steps needed to be. He would head to the garden center first thing this morning and apologize to Frank, and Monday morning he would try to do the same to Eric.

Less than an hour later, Kevin was exiting his car, working his way through the parking lot in hopes that Frank would be working. His excitement at seeing Frank again caught him by surprise, and he realized that he had been so preoccupied with himself that he hadn't even considered that it might be Frank's day off. Kevin didn't worry for long because Frank was making an immediate beeline for him.

Frank called over, "Kevin, what brings you back today?" His gravelly voice was warm with affection.

"Frank, good morning. I uh, I wanted to apologize. It's something I don't do often." Shame welled up in Kevin. "You asked me a question earlier this week, and I uh…I just walked away. I left because I couldn't handle it, and I'm sorry Frank. It was a mistake, and you didn't deserve that."

Frank looked warmly at him for a moment, then quickly brushed the whole thing off. "Nonsense, young man. You came back, and that's all that matters." He paused. "Walk with me for a minute."

They walked through the crowd in silence for some time, the beauty of the garden holding Kevin's attention completely.

As they neared the back of the property, where the only sounds were sprinklers and misting machines, Frank finally broke the silence. "Last week, you asked what people needed to thrive, and I asked you why you wanted to know. My question stands, Kevin. Why do you want to know? Who are you fighting for? Your son, your team—are you fighting for them, or are you fighting for yourself?"

By now, they had made their way outside, towards the fruit trees and berry bushes. The crowds thinned the further they walked.

Kevin looked at the ground. He had anticipated this moment but didn't have the right words.

"I don't know anymore," he said. He felt wetness forming in the corners of his eyes. "I'm tired, Frank. Tired of fighting. Tired of conflict. Tired of working so hard and feeling the things that matter most are slipping through my hands.

"I'm a selfish man, Frank. I push, and I work…I want to fight for my son. I want my team to be happy, but I don't know how to make them happy. I don't know what to do anymore."

Kevin continued to meet Frank's gaze. He was facing his

The Leader's Garden

inner demons and wanted Frank to know he wasn't going to shy away from them. Not this time. He wiped his eyes, but this time, he didn't push the emotions down or try to deflect them. Instead, he just breathed a few heavy breaths and gave himself a second to recover.

Frank nodded and smiled. "Well. That's something we can work with," he said, patting Kevin on the back with what felt like a fatherly gesture and caused an involuntary tensing in Kevin, who wasn't accustomed to comforting gestures in situations like this.

"Son, I'm going to share with you all I know about growing healthy people. I didn't come by this knowledge lightly, and I don't share it easily. I'm going to give it to you, and freely, but before I do, I am going to need a commitment from you."

Kevin's focused his attention completely on Frank, hanging on his every word. As he listened, he realized he was no longer concerned with whether or not Frank had true wisdom to share. More than ever, he was convinced that he had made the right decision in coming back. Relief washed over him.

Frank, who continued on. "I'm going to share with you but only if you commit to me that no matter what your brain tells you, no matter how awkward it might feel, you're going to implement what I tell you, exactly the way I tell you. Those are my terms, son. You can take 'em or leave 'em."

The old man looked Kevin in the eye and thrust his weathered hand out. Without hesitation, Kevin locked eyes with Frank, gave him his word, and sealed it all with a handshake. The silence and cool morning air were the only witnesses to the deal that had just been made.

"Alright then, let's get to it," Frank said.

Kevin felt like Frank was informing his new student that class had officially begun.

Kevin reached into his pocket and pulled out his phone, but before he could open *Notes*, Frank cut him off with a laugh. "Am I boring you already?"

"Not at all. Taking notes," Kevin shot back excitedly.

The Leader's Garden

"Put that thing away. This is going to be simple enough to remember without notes. Besides, the best lessons are often the simplest lessons, the kind you can commit to memory immediately!

"So, let's start with this. How would you describe what we've been doing together so far, Kevin?"

Kevin thought for a moment. "Talking, I suppose."

"Good. That's good. And you're right, we have been talking. But we've been spending something, too. Something finite. Something neither of us will ever get back. It's the most precious thing either of us has to give, and it's something we can never reclaim or earn more of, no matter how hard we might try."

"Time," Kevin answered, picking up on the answer right away.

"Exactly," Frank said without missing a beat. "Plants need three things to thrive, and the first is good soil; people need three things to thrive, and the first is our time. Never forget that people know how important they are to us by how much of it we give them. Like our money, we spend our time on the things we value, and we should look at every moment spent as an investment. When investing, we can be wise or foolish, intentional or unintentional. No matter the case, in the end it will all be spent, every last minute."

"Ok. I think I get it," Kevin replied.

"Not yet, you don't," Frank shot back. "Talk to me about the time you spend with your son."

Instantly, Kevin tensed up as self-preservation overwhelmed him and shame tried to bubble up to the surface. Even though his cheeks reddened, he forced himself to push through. "I...uh...Well, last night I spent some time helping him with his homework, and I drive him to jiu-jitsu twice a week. And sometimes on the weekend..." he trailed off, losing his words. "Honestly, I don't know what to say."

He looked at Frank, searching for judgment in his eyes, but he only found sympathy and understanding.

The Leader's Garden

"I understand, son. More than you know. Believe it or not, I wasn't always a gardener. My wife and I, rest her soul, struggled through the early years of our marriage, and raising kids isn't meant to be easy. Rewarding things never are."

Frank paused for a moment, and Kevin wondered if he was remembering a lifetime gone by.

He picked up again. "Imagine our relationship as a rope, Kevin. A braided rope made up of innumerable individual cords. Depending on the strength of our bond, the rope can be thick as a bridge's suspension or thin as a braided wire. Now imagine this rope anchors us together. What if every time I let you down or you and I have conflict, when I'm hard on you or lose my temper, I take a knife to that cord. Over time, little by little, I fray or cut thread after thread. Now imagine that process happening again and again over the course of our relationship, over the course of a lifetime."

Frank smiled and nodded as he saw the concept sinking in. "If I am not careful, I can cut too many cords, slice too many threads. When that happens and the weight of the relationship gets to be too much for the cord to bear...SNAP, we fall apart."

Frank held Kevin's attention so thoroughly that Kevin visibly flinched on the "SNAP."

"Now think about your son, Kevin, and think about your team. What do their cords look like? Are they thicker than an elephant's trunk, strong enough to withstand a storm, or are they more like strands of yarn being blown in the wind?"

Kevin understood the analogy. The relationships in his life were hanging by a thread, and he never seemed to find time to do anything about it. He liked to think he was treading water, but he was clearly sinking instead.

"Now don't look so down, son," Frank nudged, "All's not lost. Just because you damage the cord doesn't mean it stays that way! In fact, you're going to start repairing that cord tonight."

Kevin's eyebrows raised with doubt reflexively, his skeptical thoughts showing through. For years, he had operated on the presupposition that when relationships became too damaged, there was simply nothing that could be done. It was a fundamental belief imparted to him by his father during the divorce and one he had been unable to shake off.

"Trust me. Adding threads to that cord is as easy as spending time wisely, and I'm going to give you the secret to fighting that war on two fronts. The first front, which I'm guessing comes naturally to you, is in the practical doing. It's about all of the things you do to help people. It's when you're there for them, and it's when you keep your word and show them that they can count on you for help. Think about all the things you do to train your people at work or when you help your boy with his homework or when you work on projects together.

"I don't care if you're coaching, training, or digging trenches beside them, every time you spend your effort and brainpower on others, you're adding to the cord. It's that simple. Are you understanding so far?"

Kevin was certain repairing relationships wasn't as simple as Frank made it sound, but he was still engaged and curious.

"I am, it makes sense up here," he said, tapping his temple. "But I do this, Frank. All the time. Sometimes it feels like it's all I do, and I feel like things just keep getting worse."

The trap had been sprung, and Frank pounced. "It's getting worse, Kevin, because this is only half of the equation and it is ALL you do. You're not focusing enough on the second front in this war, and that's where the magic happens," he paused a moment then asked quizzically, "do you like chips and salsa?"

"I'm sorry?" Kevin asked, confused.

"Chips and salsa," Frank insisted.

Kevin replied, "Yeah, I mean, of course. Who doesn't?"

"Good. You're going to start eating a lot of it." Frank's tone was serious, and it seemed as if he expected Kevin to just get the allusion.

"Chips and salsa?" Kevin asked, still bewildered. "You lost me."

The Leader's Garden

"You're good at spending time ON people Kevin. It's time for you to start spending more time WITH people. Sure, you help your boy with his homework, but when was the last time you sat on the porch and talked about nothing just to wait for the sun to set and the stars to shine? When was the last time you talked about football over coffee or some good old-fashioned chips and salsa for no reason at all?"

Kevin thought quietly, then replied, "I don't know. It's been a while, I guess."

"And I'm guessing it's even less with your team. Spending time on people is great, son. Aren't many better ways to use your time I can think of, save one. Spending time with them. If you think about that cord holding your relationship together, those individual strings are no good on their own. You've got to braid them together if you want them to hold. They need to be both strong and thick because they're going to take a lot of damage over a lifetime. If they can't survive the storm, you'll lose them forever."

"That makes sense," Kevin said under his breath.

He was thinking about how he had gotten this so wrong and how thin the cords in his relationships must be.

"Listen, you're going to make mistakes. You're going to say the wrong thing. It's the beauty of the human condition that we can improve on our mistakes and keep getting better! You've made a mess of things, you've let things get out of control, but these relationships can be saved. You're the secret to making that happen.

"I promise you that for starters, the more time you spend with them, the thicker and stronger their cords are going to get. Strong cords mean strong bonds, and strong bonds mean strong relationships."

Kevin reflected, *Is this where I'm coming up short? I'm not spending enough time with them? I mean, how much time am I expected to spend with people during the work day? We have a job to do.* But Kevin also realized strong relationships and trust went hand-in-hand, and both were foundational to high-performing teams.

Frank continued on, "Now assuming that's sunk in, I reckon it's time for you to get out of here so you can stop by the store on your way back."

Kevin looked at Frank quizzically for a moment. He was about to ask a question when the lightbulb went on.

The two of them said in unison, "Chips and salsa."

A short while later, after stopping at the store, Kevin thought about his relationship with Frank and realized that the man had been modeling this lesson since the moment they met. He had been building a cord by spending time on him and with him, and that cord was already strong enough to withstand their first storm.

Without a second thought, Kevin committed to putting this principle into practice with Eric on Monday.

==========The Big Idea==========

Time is the most valuable resource we have to give. Where money can be earned, spent, invested, and multiplied, time is given to each of us in a fixed amount. Outside of healthy eating, exercise, and generally adopting good habits, there is little any of us can do to extend the amount of time we are allotted. On top of that, even when each of those things is done to perfection, rich or poor, we still only have twenty-four hours to spend each day.

Due in no small part to its inherent scarcity, one of the primary ways that people know how much they mean to us is by the amount of time we spend with them.

==========Exercise==========

Consider at least three people at work/home that you are responsible for and answer the following questions:

1. On a scale of 1-10, by your estimate, how strong would THEY say your relationship is? Don't forget that you can always ask directly!
2. On a scale of 1-10, how challenging is their current situation/stage of development?
3. Roughly how much time do you spend with them each week in hours, and is it enough?

CHAPTER 5
Reflection

"The best relationship is where yesterday's fight doesn't stop today's communication" Unknown

Earlier in this book, I introduced the idea that just like plants need soil, water, and sunlight, people need three things to thrive. We now know that the first of these three is time. Time is the thing people need more from us than anything else. Our time is our most valuable resource, and as Frank said, we can spend it wisely or foolishly, intentionally or unintentionally, but in the end, each of us will spend every last minute of it.

When we choose to invest our time in others, there are various ways that we can go about doing it. One way is by spending it on practical things, like helping with homework or doing household chores. Unfortunately, helping people with their problems directly doesn't always automatically show them that we care about them, nor does caring about someone emotionally naturally show them that they can lean on and depend on us.

To simplify things, we first have to split time invested into two main categories: Formal Time and Informal Time. Formal Time is spent helping people with their problems, be they relational or professional. It is time spent working together, providing feedback and advice, or doing things like teaching, coaching, mentoring, or apprenticing. Formal Time is practical time spent on practical things.

On the other hand, Informal Time is time spent simply being together. Frank introduced the idea through simple chips and salsa, something any of us can buy at the store for as little as a few dollars. When applied properly, talking over chips and salsa can be worth more than its weight in relational gold. Some simple examples of Informal Time are things like chatting on the porch, playing board games, reading stories to your children, having lunch with your people, checking in over morning coffee, or calling your spouse for no reason other than to say "hi." Understanding your family or team will help you choose Informal Time activities that will have the greatest return, but when in doubt, chips and salsa never fail!

When considering Formal and Informal Time, note that there is no one-size-fits-all formula for people. Every human being needs a different combination of Formal and Informal Time based on their personality and the situation and stage of life they find themselves in. There are, however, a few guidelines we can use to help us when all else fails.

For starters, when someone is struggling to complete a task, is buried under work, or is going through a situation they are unfamiliar with, spending Formal Time helping them through their problem is wise. You can do so by assisting them in outlining a plan, directing them to resources, and, yes, even taking some of their burden on as part of your own if you have the capacity.

When someone is going through a frustrating season, is feeling down on themselves, or is dealing with any interpersonal conflict or drama, increasing the amount of Informal Time you are spending on them is a good idea. One simple gesture is to invite them to coffee and commit to doing twice as much listening as talking. Other examples of Informal Time are simple phone calls, watching movies, going to sporting events, or rounds of miniature golf.

In the end, Formal Time is all about the practical and helping people in tangible ways, while Informal Time is all about the connection, and helping people see that they are valued! Before we move on, understand that knowing the needs of those we lead is only the first half of the equation. The second half is knowing ourselves. Just like everyone needs a different calibration of Formal and Informal Time, each of us has a natural tendency to lean into either Informal or Formal Time. What I mean by that is that one of the two comes more naturally to us and is easier for us to invest. It is also likely to be the one we value more and need more from others. The downside is that we often are not quite as good at investing the other in people and are far more likely to value it less.

For me personally, I am a self-proclaimed master at Formal Time. There is no problem I won't stick my nose into, and I am a wannabe expert in virtually all topics, so I am confident enough to trample on any conversation even if I only heard half a sentence or two. The plus side is that people often come to me when they need help solving problems, and I am typically quite good at helping them figure out what to do.

The downside is that I tend to be blind to the relational damage I cause. Informal Tme, on the other hand, is often awkward for me, and I have a tendency to avoid it when I can. My preference for Formal Time causes me to forgo building and restoring relationships on a regular basis, which can lead to hurt feelings and unnecessary conflict with the people that matter most in my life.

What about you? Do you find that it is more natural for you to help people with their problems, or do you prefer to spend time enjoying the company of others? If you don't know, imagine I came into your office upset about something that happened. Is your natural reaction to provide comfort and empathy or to try and fix the problem? Those of us that are naturally more adept at Formal Time tend to be problem solvers. Those of us that are naturally more adept at Informal Time tend to be more empathetic.

CHAPTER 6
Chips & Salsa

"Eric, can we talk?" Kevin felt foolish and awkward standing in the door of Eric's office holding a grocery bag of chips and salsa.

He wondered how things had gotten this way. The last thing Kevin wanted was for this relationship to continue deteriorating, and so he was ready to apologize, wholly and unconditionally.

Eric, his eyes on his desk, beat Kevin to the punch. "Kevin, I'm sorry for—"

"Stop. Just stop right there," Kevin cut him off. "Everything you said, all of it, was true. I'm sorry I needed to hear it so badly, and I'm sorry you had to be the one to tell me." He kept on, "I know you work for me, but Eric, I've always wanted us to be friends, and honestly, I've been doing a pretty lousy job of treating you like one lately."

Kevin was stunned at how eager he was to get these words out. His naturally defensive nature and desire for justice were surprisingly absent this morning. "I'm sorry I haven't been checking in on you, and I came in here to ask your forgiveness..."

The Leader's Garden

Eric was now looking at him with what seemed like hope and a little admiration.

Kevin held up the bag he was holding. "I even brought a peace offering. Chips and salsa?"

Eric smiled warmly and returned the question with a "Sure!"

He moved his chair to a better angle for conversation. Kevin sat across from him, pulled the food from the bag, and put the items on the table.

After passing the salsa to Eric, he opened the bag of chips and said jokingly, "Now, I don't want to pull seniority here, but I'm putting a no double-dipping rule in place. Company policy."

Eric cocked his head and gave a chuckle.

"Fair enough," he said, then dipped his first chip.

The two made small talk for a good ten minutes or so, discussing trends in cyber-security. As the conversation hit a stride, Kevin watched Eric intently and realized for the first time that the man looked considerably older and less rested than usual.

Kevin kicked himself for not considering that something might be going on with him. *Have I been this self-absorbed?* he wondered.

Without thinking twice, he interrupted Eric mid-sentence. "Eric, what's going on with you? I'm worried, and sitting here, I can't help but feel like I should have been worried about you a while ago."

The question interrupted the flow of the conversation, but if it caught Eric by surprise, he didn't show it.

He stated flatly, "Kyree and I have decided to separate for a little while. Things just aren't going well."

"Eric, I'm so sorry. That's horrible."

Kevin and Julie had been to dinner with the two of them more than once, and Kevin had never seen anything indicating a separation was coming. If things were this bad, he realized that there was a good possibility that either he hadn't been paying attention or they had just been hiding it really well—which still might just mean he hadn't cared enough to pay attention.

The Leader's Garden

"No, don't be. It's not you or work at all. This has been going on for a while before I came on here. I want it all to work out. I think she does, too. We just need to get it all sorted. In the meantime, I've been staying in a hotel. There have been a few days where getting out of bed just hasn't been possible."

A lump welled up in Kevin's throat just thinking about Eric lying in bed alone, dealing with the heartbreak he was going through. Though he was overwhelmed by sympathy, part of him was terrified that his own marriage might be headed off a cliff.

"Eric, I am so sorry. Why didn't you say anything?" Kevin asked.

Eric took a few seconds before responding. "Honestly, I don't know. I mean, I trust my team. I know they have my back. I knew that everyone would feel bad and want to help, but I didn't want anyone else to know what I've been going through.

"If I said it out loud, that meant it was real, and I don't know if I'm ready to accept that yet myself. I'm sorry, I should have said something. I see that now." Eric stated the last part matter-of-factly.

Kevin accepted the apology but wasn't about to let the responsibility rest on Eric's shoulders alone. "We all made mistakes, Eric. I'm sorry I wasn't paying enough attention to see the change in you. That's part of my job, and more than that, I've been letting myself become someone I don't want to be. I'm trying hard to do something about it. That's what the chips and salsa were all about—a small gesture to let you know I want to be better...to do better.

"I want you to know I'm committed to you. We're committed to you. I know Julie would say the same thing." Even with their fights, Kevin knew that Julie had a heart for him and the people he worked with. "We're going to do whatever we can to help you through this. You can count on us."

Eric's mouth opened as if to talk, but emotion seemed to overcome him, so Kevin raised a hand up and stopped him.

"No need to say anything." He stood up and extended the hand to Eric, who returned the handshake firmly. "We're in this together, Eric. You're not going through this alone, not anymore."

With that, Kevin offered to clean up the food and left the office feeling decidedly better than when he had walked in.

==

That afternoon, Kevin was raring to get out of work and get home before any of his family got there. He had another bag of chips and salsa in his car, and he was ready to see if the magic in the bag was going to work its wonders on his relationship with his son.

Kevin was sitting in the living room tapping his foot as Anthony burst through the door. Anthony dropped his bag by the front door and headed up towards his room.

"Anthony, hold up," Kevin called.

Anthony stopped in his tracks, startled. Kevin realized he had probably scared his son half to death.

Anthony's voice was shocked but measured when he called down, "Dad? You scared the heck out of me. What are you doing here?"

"I came home early, buddy. To hang out with you." He held up the grocery bag eagerly, as if it spoke for itself.

Looking at the bag himself, Kevin realized he wasn't being entirely clear.

Before Kevin could clarify what he meant, Anthony started down the stairs with a skeptical look on his face. "What's that? Groceries?"

Kevin felt a little flustered. *What's wrong with me?* He wanted to connect with his son so badly. He loved Anthony more than anything in the world, but every sentence was forced and came out mixed up. "No. I mean, yes. But. Chips." He paused, once again leaving out the point entirely. "Chips and Salsa. Do you want some? With me, I mean?"

His internal voice told him to run. *Oh, this is hopeless!*

He finally forced the words out, "Sit down, I want to have

some chips and salsa with you."

Whew.

Anthony, likely concerned at seeing his dad home alone at this hour, must have thought a talk was coming and asked with caution in his voice, "Are you ok? Am I in trouble? Did you get fired or something?"

Kevin, still a little flustered, replied, "No. Who's going to fire me, Anthony? We own the company, and no you're not in trouble."

Kevin's thoughts were finally starting to settle, and though he still felt a little unlike himself, he tried to get the conversation back under control. "I came home early to see you. I just wanted to hang out and share some chips and salsa with my son."

"Are you and mom getting a divorce?" Anthony asked almost sarcastically.

Kevin let that one go with extreme intentionality. He wasn't going to get derailed again and risk losing Anthony entirely.

"No, absolutely not. Come on, son. Sit down."

The two settled into their chairs and sat in awkward silence for a few long seconds.

Surprisingly, Anthony was the first to break it, "So..."

Kevin, not sure what to say, took the cue, "So..." He paused, then said, "How was school today?"

Anthony shrugged. He bit off most of a chip and said between bites, "Good, I guess."

Kevin ate a chip of his own, not quite sure what to say next. "So, any big plans this weekend?"

The conversation went on more or less like that for the next fifteen to twenty minutes or so before Anthony asked to be excused so he could do his homework. Kevin wasn't sure if he should be offended but decided to count the whole thing as a win and just let it go. On the one hand, it had been pretty awkward, and they really didn't have much to talk about. On the other hand, Anthony had sat with him, even hung out for a while without complaining.

Even though talking over chips and salsa wasn't going to be a cure-all for their strained relationship, it was a start. It was a window into his son's life, and Kevin was going to start fighting to keep that window open...maybe even upgrade to a door someday.

==

Later that night, Julie didn't look up from her book as Kevin came to bed. When Kevin joined her, there was no tense silence as had been the norm lately. Instead, he climbed into bed, sat upright, and waited patiently for Julie to acknowledge him. Though he was proud of the efforts he had made that day, he wasn't seeking praise. If anything, he was excited to have things to share that demonstrated effort towards improving their lives.

Julie, seemingly oblivious, flipped to the next page, then surprised him. Without looking up from her book, she said, "Alright, out with it. What's going on?"

"Julie, Eric's separated from his wife...temporarily I guess, but it's not looking good," Kevin said.

Julie put her book down, concern etched across her face. "Oh, that's horrible."

Once again, shame welled up in Kevin as he thought about his mistakes. "Honestly, I feel like an idiot. I didn't find out about it until today, and only then because I laid into him for missing work last week."

"Oh, Kevin," Julie replied with a mix of sadness and disappointment, "how'd that go over?"

"I burned through a lot of chips and salsa today, I'll tell you that," he said, his words stated like an inside joke.

Julie paused, likely trying to digest the reference.

Eventually, she asked, "Chips and salsa?"

"Oh, yeah, I'm trying something new. Let me explain. You know how it always feels like I'm somewhere else? How you say I'm present but not really present?"

Julie nodded slowly with what appeared to be skepticism.

"Well, I met Eric in his office today, apologized and made a peace offering...something to take some of the awkwardness away, something everyone loves..." he paused, silently offering to let her fill in the blank.

"Chips and salsa..." Julie played along.

He kept at it, building enthusiasm. He was like a kid with a new toy or a carpenter with a new tool. "Right. We had a fiesta right there in his office—"

Julie cut him off before he got another word out. "Back up half a step. So you're telling me you initiated an apology without me having to use secret ninja pressure points on you? What's going on with you?"

Kevin wasn't quite ready to share all he was going through, as he wanted to take a little more time to sort through how he felt and what he planned to do.

"Want to hear the craziest part?" Kevin teased.

Julie said in mock-surprise, "There's more?"

"Yeah, I actually left work early today and had some chips and salsa with Anthony, if you can believe that." Kevin was practically beaming.

Julie cocked her head as if she had heard him wrong. "You left work...AND spent time, ALONE, with Anthony. Do you have cancer, Kevin?"

He smiled, his voice growing more patient with each word. "No. Nothing's wrong. I'm just...You said I needed to make some changes, and I'm trying. I know it's one day, but there's something here I don't want to lose. I have to try...to fight."

She listened, though her face didn't match the hope on his. It was one day, after all.

Kevin's face relaxed considerably as he tried to explain his reasoning to her. "I don't want to feel hopeless anymore, Julie. I don't want to feel helpless. Something has to be done, and I have to be the one to do it. I refuse to believe there's nothing I can do."

Kevin knew Julie well enough to know that tackling these issues on his own, without her prompting him, was the last thing she had expected from her husband. He knew she wouldn't be ready to jump on board and believe he was a new man overnight, and honestly, he wasn't. But he also knew that she did love him very much, and that meant that their marriage was still very much worth fighting for!

"There's always something you can do, Kevin. We all love you. We just want to get your best, that's all. I'm glad Anthony got it today. Let's see what happens tomorrow." She tousled his hair playfully.

"Let's see, indeed," Kevin responded with a smirk that showed he was up to the challenge.

==========The Big Idea==========

Of all things in your life, relationships are worth fighting for the most. Where virtually everything else can be bought, sold, replaced, or traded, relationships can be none of these things. The more money we have, the harder it is to tell who around us values us rather than the opportunities we provide. The more power we acquire, the harder it is to tell who is laughing at our jokes because we are funny and who is trying to please us.

Relationships, on the other hand, are priceless. They are one of a kind, unique by their very nature. While we can expand our networks over time, our oldest relationships have the deepest roots and prove to be the most sentimental long term as the stories we share with those we have known the longest often occupy a place in our minds and hearts that virtually nothing else comes close to.

==========Exercise==========

Spend time reflecting on the relationships at home/work and answer the following questions:
1. Are there any relationships that have become damaged where you are even 10% at fault?
2. If yes, write out an apology focusing solely on your responsibility in the situation without mentioning theirs.
3. Then, make one of three choices: burn it, file it, or send it. Once you finish, email me at chipsandsalsa@marktilsher.com with the subject line Chips & Salsa and let me know which one you chose!

CHAPTER 6
Reflection

"When you realize you've made a mistake, make amends immediately. It's easier to eat crow while it's still warm." Dan Heist

Making the first move is something I have never been good at. For example, while we were courting, or so I thought, I was under the impression that my wife-to-be and I had been dating for over a year, while she simply thought we were good friends. I had been working up the courage to make my move for so long that she was completely oblivious to the fact that I was even interested in her.

A good rule of thumb when it comes to making the first move in damaged relationships or when growing healthy, high-performing people is to "be the grownup." Let me explain. While I am proud of my relationships with my children, there are times (more than I would like to admit) that I bring less than my "A Game" to the table. Conversely, like all human beings, my children are not always the best versions of themselves, and inevitably one of us ends up stepping on the other's toes or causing offense.

When it comes to my children, as the grownup, I ALWAYS bear the responsibility to make the first move! Regardless of whether they caused the offense or I did, there is virtually no situation where I should sit back and wait for them to approach me first. I say "virtually" because there are times when we may deliberately step back and let them process or use the opportunity to train them up, but as a general rule, the grownup must move first!

I personally find this rule to be one of the simplest I teach people but also the most difficult to implement personally. My default gear is prideful arrogance, and when left to my nature, I want the world to conform to me and to right its own wrongs before it expects me to right mine. Unfortunately, when both sides in a conflict refuse to humble themselves and make the first move, they may never get the opportunity to reconcile, and the relationship may stay damaged or even atrophy. I have personally lost more than one relationship because both sides refused to take a single step towards the other, and this sad reality continues to cause negative repercussions year after year.

This conundrum doesn't apply solely to personal relationships either. So many of our AMAZING leaders tout their open-door policies with pride. They believe themselves approachable, and truly they may be, but, by the very nature of the hierarchy, simply opening your door and waiting for the wounded to pour through is a recipe for disaster.

There are far too many of us that will nurse even fatal wounds alone, dying before we dream of asking anyone else for help. Keep your open-door policy, celebrate it even! But alone, it is not enough. Imagine running your home with an open-door policy and letting everyone in the house know that they are free to approach you at any time. Would you assume everything was ok because no one brought up any issues?

The idea of an open-door policy alone is no less preposterous at work! You may leave your office door open, and month after month, year after year, your subordinates smile when they walk by and never enter your office with any meaningful problems. Again, should we assume everything is ok because no one approached us to tell us that it wasn't?

Many studies have been done on employee engagement, and one of my favorites, "State of the American Manager" comes from Gallup. In it, the researchers studied manager engagement, which they defined as "those who are involved in, enthusiastic about and committed to their work and workplace."

One of my key takeaways from their findings was that the way employees rated two statements, had an overwhelming impact on engagement. The first statement was "I feel I can talk with my manager about nonwork-related issues," and the second was "I feel I can approach my manager with any type of question." For employees that answered "no" to these two questions, 92% and 98% identified themselves as disengaged. These are employees that are either intentionally or unintentionally not giving their best, or worse, are not only seeking other jobs but may be sabotaging you from the inside either outright or through malicious compliance. The key takeaway for me here is that our employees, those we lead, must be able to answer YES to both of these questions if we want them to be highly involved and enthusiastic about their work and workplace.

Open door policies will not and cannot foster this level of communication. We must actively and intentionally spend Informal Time with our people if we want to expand on the types of questions and problems they can bring to our attention. Ignore these findings at your own peril.

With this newfound knowledge, I encourage you to use Formal Time judiciously and help your people with their problems, ensure they are being trained, and address their concerns. At the same time, heap Informal Time on those you are entrusted with, and not only will they become more engaged, your relationship will change as you watch them grow towards you as plants grow towards sunlight.

CHAPTER 7

What Do You See?

Kevin was swamped that week. He was being pulled in a thousand directions, being everything to everyone. At work they had had onboarded two new clients and hired a new quality assurance tech; and at home they had started digging out the retaining wall for Anthony's project. Still, Kevin found ways to be intentional, if only for a few minutes each day. He kept dropping in on Eric, and even though Anthony was coming along begrudgingly, the two of them had been spending more and more time together each day.

Kevin had started spending a few minutes in Anthony's room before bed each night just to check in, and while there wasn't a lot to talk about at first, he was starting to recognize that his son might be looking forward to those few minutes at the end of the day. With all of this going on, it was Thursday before he had the whitespace on his calendar to get back to see Frank again.

Because Kevin went so late in the day, Frank was swamped with regular customers and couldn't rush over to greet him. Kevin was forced to wait for the man's attention. Eventually, the two of them were walking and talking about their families

The Leader's Garden

and the weeks they had had, and then they shared a few laughs outside near the fruit trees on two decorative boulders.

As the conversation hit a lull, Kevin asked, "Sure has been hot hasn't it?"

Frank didn't seem pleased with Kevin bringing up the weather and replied immediately, "Let's skip the mall talk, tell me, how did it go?"

Kevin returned the impatience with a smile of his own. "Good. Good. It went...Well."

Again, Frank seemed enthusiastic about moving the conversation forward. "Well, of course it went well. That much is visible on your face. I'm going to need a little more detail than that, though. I grew up on radio, son. You're going to have to paint me a word picture."

"Ok, ok. Well, I'm out of chips and salsa." Kevin replied with a laugh. "Anthony and I talked. We've talked more than once this week actually. Not sure it's making a difference, but it's happening. The first day, he thought that I had bad news, that maybe his mom and I were getting divorced or he was in trouble, but he's starting to loosen up a little, I think."

Frank listened intently, a proud smile slowly spreading across his face. He put his hand on Kevin's shoulder, giving it a good squeeze. Kevin accepted the gesture and even patted Frank on the back in kind even if it still felt a bit unnatural for him.

"You see," Frank said, "you can do this. I'm sure it wasn't perfect, but it never is, is it? The important thing is to get momentum and hold onto it like a tiger's tail. Fight for that time, and protect it! Guard it from the outside world like it matters to you!"

"You're right," Kevin said, "and I can't thank you enough, Frank. I feel like a different man already, even if they don't see it yet. You've given me hope, a second chance to fix all of this."

Frank failed to fight back a sad look, as if he saw something Kevin didn't, but it passed almost as quickly as it appeared, and Kevin was none the wiser. Frank cleared his throat. "There's more than a chance, son. You will fix all this. The fact that your boy sat with you and talked means you haven't lost him yet. You're his father, so let's help you be the best one you can be!"

Kevin nodded slowly, agreeing silently.

The two continued walking together in silence, Kevin waiting patiently while Frank sorted his thoughts. "You know, my son and I didn't talk for nearly twenty-five years after I got back from the Vietnam War. It wasn't always easy back then…" He paused, overcome by something Kevin couldn't see or begin to comprehend.

When he spoke again, Kevin felt like Frank was trying to avoid talking about the war altogether and wanted to change the subject. "Well, I came back a different man, to say the least, and the war didn't end when I got home either. When my son had enough, I had to learn all these lessons the hard way."

Kevin wasn't sure how to respond to the revelations from Frank's past. Frank spoke so little about himself and his own family that Kevin assumed he didn't want to, and now he was getting a glimpse of why.

"I'm…I'm sorry, Frank," Kevin said.

"Oh no, now don't be. I made out better than most, and there is a lot to be grateful for. Just look around. I've lived a good life, a great life, and those problems went under the bridge a long, long time ago. You would have liked my son, Charles. He was a lot like you in a lot of ways. He was a good man. He just had to find his own way, that's all."

Frank took a deep breath and wiped his face with his handkerchief. Whether to wipe sweat or tears, Kevin couldn't tell. All Kevin knew was that this moment was solemn and meant a lot to Frank, so he gave the moment the silence it deserved.

Frank took off his glasses and began polishing them with his handkerchief. "Now the office. Eric, how's that one getting along?"

Kevin felt that old shame welling up again while self-preservation was trying to pull him down, but this time he refused to give it a voice. Instead, he countered the negative thoughts with a deep breath and a long, slow sigh.

"Man, I really botched that one, Frank. Can you believe that my number one guy was missing work and acting the opposite of his normal self, and all I thought to do was let him have it? He's having trouble at home with his wife. It's not looking good. I think I just might have been the biggest idiot on the planet."

Frank chuckled at that, not confirming it but leaving it in the air seemingly to toy with Kevin, which caused him to stop talking about Eric and focus on Frank instead.

"You know, you really are something, Frank. There's just something about you I can't quite put my finger on. You're like Yoda or Adrian in Rocky. There's a lot going on up there, isn't there?" The comments came out with a laugh. "You got me to apologize. I even made the first move. It was awkward, but I did it, and God bless him, he forgave me. I literally yelled at him during the toughest time of his life, and he tried apologizing to me.

"And before you say anything, I know it's not about me, but I do want to be there for him, and truly, I thought I had lost him. I thought there was nothing I could do..."

"Oh, there's always something you can do, son," Frank chimed in without missing a beat.

His eyes twinkled with more pride for him than Kevin had seen in the eyes of another man in his entire life.

By now, it was around noon, and they were under the sun in the open air. Frank looked up at the sky as if scanning for the source of the sweltering heat. "Well, I'm proud of you, Kevin. You took the first step. But it's just the first step, nothing more. The real challenge comes in staying the course, but you already know that, don't you?"

Kevin held his lips together but nodded along slowly.

Frank kept at it. "A few days ago, you made a commitment to me, and I'm going to hold you to it. You're going to see this thing through to the very end, you hear? You better buy some stock in tortilla chips because we're about to make some investors rich."

On that, Frank grabbed a watering can and headed over to a nearby spigot. He moved so quickly, Kevin almost got left behind. By the time he caught up, Frank was already filling the can with one hand and dipping his handkerchief in the water with the other. He held the dripping cloth out to Kevin, motioning for him to wipe his forehead with it. Kevin tried to wave it off politely but did little to hide the surprise on his face at being offered the dirty rag. Frank shrugged, turned off the spigot, and set the can down in a shady spot.

Taking a deep breath, he lowered down into a squat, resting his forearms on his legs, and something about looking down at Frank felt wrong to Kevin, so within a second or two, he was squatting down in the shade as well. Squatting here in silence with Frank, Kevin had a minute to really appreciate the beauty of the outdoor space and its sprawling, natural landscaping. Kevin couldn't believe he and his family weren't coming out here just to walk the property.

Kevin wasn't sure if he was supposed to be the next one to talk, but he felt like breaking the silence would somehow spoil the moment, so he kept silent, even when he started to feel awkward.

Frank didn't seem to even notice, though, and broke through the silence like a sledgehammer, seemingly starting at the end of a thought rather than the beginning, "I believe in you, Kevin."

He then stopped talking as quickly as he had started. Because neither had spoken in so long, and Kevin wasn't even looking at Frank, the words startled him. When Kevin looked back, the sad look he had missed earlier was there on Frank's face.

"I see the man in you that you don't see yet, and I see the troubles you still have yet ahead of you. I know it's hard to see past the moment sometimes, beyond today's problems. That's maybe the only good part of nearing the end of your life: *perspective*. I've got the benefit of looking back at a lifetime of experience.

"After a while, you start to see pretty clearly how the story ends before you even make it past the first chapter. I'll be honest, some stories aren't worth reading. They play off the same old tropes, and if you've seen one, sometimes you feel like you've seen them all.

"In some stories, the hero never makes it across the finish line. Their stories never get told because they fail to rise to the challenge and confront their own demons. Honestly, I thought you might be one of the ones that fail to rise to the challenge when I first met you. But not anymore...not anymore. I was wrong about you.

"I can see that now. I see the end of your story, Kevin. I see what you can't see yet. Heck, the best part of being young is you don't know how the story ends. There are endless possibilities ahead of you. You've got youth. You've got health. You've got vigor. I can see your story, Kevin, and as far as I can tell, it's going to be a damn good one. And I reckon, if you play your cards just right, your family is going to get the happy ending they deserve."

"Really?" Kevin muttered almost inaudibly.

"Really," Frank smiled. "But don't mistake me, I'm not saying it won't be painful—dying to yourself always is. It's about the most difficult thing you can do. It's painful, but I promise you, in the end, it's worth it. Believe me, it's worth it. The rewards are greater than you can imagine.

"Only when you truly lay your own life down do you have a chance to gain it. It's the mystery everyone out there is still trying desperately to figure out. But not you. You've gotten a taste, and I believe that's going to be enough to keep you going. You will get through this, and soon, very soon, you're going to have a team people will be fighting to get on, not one where folks are struggling to hang on. More than that, you're going to have a family overflowing, one that can give from abundance."

At this, Kevin's face revealed some of his inner skepticism, which Frank seemed to note immediately.

"Like I said, you can't see it. You don't need to see it. Not yet. But you will, and soon I hope," he said.

With that, he stood up, his cracked hands wiping dust from the front of his coveralls before he picked up the heavy watering can without so much as a grunt.

Kevin, dumbstruck, wasn't sure how to respond or what to believe. He wanted to see what Frank saw, but a round of chips and salsa with his son wasn't going to undo years of damage. Kevin wanted to believe, and more than that, he had committed to doing his best. Whatever happened next, he was all in. He wasn't afraid of the challenge anymore; in fact, he welcomed it!

Maybe tenacity was the solution to his problems. Maybe he had been capable before but just hadn't known WHAT to do. Frank's mentorship had given him insight that at the very least hadn't failed yet, and that was something. That was progress! Maybe the problem wasn't that everyone else around didn't understand him. Maybe how he was dealing with his problems needed to change. Maybe he needed work on both his mindset and his skillset. Maybe his head had just been trying to solve problems his heart didn't yet understand. Kevin's mind raced.

"Alright, Frank, I don't see what you see. But I believe in you. You've already done so much for me; I can't believe we are just getting started...I don't know what brought us together and why we're right here right now. But I'm committed to see this through, and I won't quit on you."

Frank returned Kevin's enthusiasm with kindness and a pat on the shoulder. "I know you won't son. I know you won't. Which leads us to our next lesson, I guess. Tell me more about Eric."

Kevin wasn't prepared for that one, and for a second it left him stumped. "He's competent, hard-working, but headstrong. Difficult, even stubborn at times. He's my friend...I think. Reliable, until recently anyway. But there's something there. Something stopping him from reaching his potential. I've never quite been able to put my finger on it. But he's broken...I can see it now. With everything going on, he's hanging on by a thread and almost ready to give up."

"I see," Frank said with a nod of understanding. "And why did you hire him?"

That was a different question entirely, one that didn't take much effort to answer. Kevin almost beamed when he started heaping praise on the young man; he saw something in Eric beyond the job he was sitting in.

"That's easy. Frank, he's a brilliant guy, brilliant! We design and install warehouse automation systems, and the man is a wizard. He can code like an absolute champion, and he isn't afraid to get his hands dirty. He'll crawl through ducts without complaint; his projects are always on time and under budget. He's a one-man show, and with a little work, he'll make a great leader. Honestly, I don't know what we would do without him," Kevin said.

"Now, tell me something," Frank continued. "If it wasn't for all the conflict, the despair, what could you do with Eric?"

Kevin responded out loud, but the words were directed at himself, as if he were thinking them for the first time. "What couldn't I do? He has unlimited potential. We're growing fast, Frank. I thought we would be regional for at least another three years, but demand is exploding. I need to hire another full team, and I'm going to need someone to train them up and head the quality control department. Beyond that, he sees the big picture. He gets it. He could be a department head, a regional director. Heck, he could replace me someday."

He stopped there, stunned he had said the words out loud.

"And there it is," Frank said with finality.

Kevin couldn't believe half of what he had just said came out of his mouth. His vision for Eric seemed so clear to him; he was surprised he had never articulated it out loud before. *He has so much potential*, Kevin thought.

Frank continued, not giving Kevin a second to breathe, "That right there, that's vision son, and it's the next lesson. You know, the Good Book says it best in Proverbs. 'Where there is no vision, the people perish.' Everything you just said to me, you need to say to him. He needs to see what you see, to see the other side of the struggle!"

Kevin visibly recoiled at the idea, but if Frank noticed, he didn't let on. He just picked up the watering can and started walking.

"Think about it, Kevin. You've got perspective. Perspective neither of them has! And that perspective can translate to vision. Vision is the spark of life, and you have it. It's in you." Beckoning to Kevin, he continued, "Keep up with me now. So, about Eric, he needs to know your vision for him, and so does your boy. Don't get me wrong, there has to be accountability as well. But, just as important, he needs to know what you see both in him and for him!"

As he talked, they rounded a corner. Frank led him through a gate in the privacy fence that separated the public space from the back of the center. Here there were trucks parked near a warehouse and loaded with mulch, large trees, and even rocks. Off to the side was a small shed, which was where Frank was leading Kevin.

"You need to talk to him about where you want your relationship to be in the short term, how you want his behavior to change, and what you're willing to give to make that happen."

Kevin felt a little uncomfortable in the employee only area, but none of the workers gave him a second glance and only greeted Frank with friendly smiles as they walked by. Eventually, Frank brought Kevin to a small worktable, which seemed to be his personal workbench as far as Kevin could tell. It was covered with basic gardening tools all meticulously arranged beside handyman tools like screwdrivers and wrenches. Two things stood out as the only decorative items on the workbench, and they were two beautiful bonsai trees.

"You know what these are?" Frank asked while he raised up his can and started watering them.

"Bonsai trees," Kevin said, happy to know the answer right away for once.

"That's right, bonsai trees," Frank said as he finished

watering them. "These two trees match a pair I keep at home, a pair I snuck back from Vietnam in the back of a C-130 Hercules. The ones at home were a gift for my wife, Allyce, and my son, and with both of them gone to rest, they're more important to me than anything else I own."

Kevin's eyes lit up with immediate recognition. "Allyce? Like Allyce's Garden Supplies? Do you own this place, Frank?"

Frank responded with what seemed to Kevin like feigned annoyance, "Well, of course, you don't think I would have called it Frank's place, did you? Now pay attention."

He picked up a pair of pruning shears and began clipping small pieces of the trees. As he did, he continued stating facts about them.

"The amazing thing about these plants is that they can grow into virtually any shape. Unlike any other plant I know of, caring for them has been elevated to an art form. People all over the world spend their lives learning to prune and shape these trees into objects of pure beauty."

He continued clipping the plants very slowly, often lining up his shears over a leaf or branch before changing his mind and forgoing the cut altogether. "I told you these two trees match the pair I brought home from Vietnam, and when I say that, I mean it. If I lined up all four of these plants right next to each other, even I would have a hard time telling the pairs apart. You know why that is?"

"Because you clipped them to match?" Kevin asked.

"Well obviously, but no. That's not the right answer, try again," Frank said with amusement.

Kevin wasn't going to be so quick to speak this time. Instead, he thought about everything Frank had said over the last few minutes. He knew he must have missed something, but that the answer was there, he just had to think about it for a second…Then, it hit him in a flash, "Vision!"

"YES!" Frank celebrated. "Vision. I have a vision for these trees. It's a vision they can't see, a vision they can't understand. But I spend time with them every day, learning them, understanding them, and, just as importantly, shaping them to suit the vision! These trees are no different than the people who need us most. When there's a vision, especially a shared vision, you can slowly work them towards their true potential both for today and someday, and believe me, both are equally important."

Frank held the shears close to a tree branch, studying it for several seconds before putting the clippers down. He continued, "Let me say it a different way: plants grow towards sunlight, people grow towards vision. It's that simple. Make sense?"

Kevin nodded. "I think so."

"Great" Frank responded. "Do you know what you have to do?"

"You know what, Frank, believe it or not, I think I do," he said, surprised at how excited he was by today's lesson.

"Me too," Frank said, and turning around, he picked up his shears and made that one final cut before walking Kevin back to the store's exit.

==

Shortly afterward, Kevin was in his car headed back to work. He replayed the conversation in his head. From the moment he got to the garden center, Frank had started pouring words of life and vision into him. By the end, it was clear he had actually been teaching Kevin a lesson the entire time, almost as if the whole situation was a setup.

"Frank, you are one crafty old man," Kevin said out loud to no one in particular.

===========**The Big Idea**===========

"A vision is not just a picture of what could be; it is an appeal to our better selves, a call to become something more." – Rosabeth Moss Kanter

To both heal and grow healthy, high-performing people, you need to provide both Time and Vision. Like Time, Vision is broken into two parts: Short-term and Long-term. Short-term Vision revolves around the immediate situation or problem, while Long-term Vision is about the potential you see in the person you're leading.

Never forget that vision is not something that is stated once and left to dangle in the ether. People need to be reminded of the collaborative, shared vision for them over and over again, especially when they have lost sight of it.

Vision reminds people that you believe in them and solidifies you as their champion, and having a champion in your corner can be the difference between success and failure, even life and death.

===========**Exercise**===========

Consider the three most important relationships in your life and reflect on these questions, then schedule time to share your vision with them:

1. Where are they right now, and where are they headed in the short term?
2. What obstacles are they dealing with right now, and how do you see them overcoming these obstacles?
3. Looking into the future, if their best qualities are allowed to develop and dominate, what will their life look like?

CHAPTER 7
Reflection

"Never assume that someone sees the light at the end of their struggle." Mark Tilsher

Take a second and read that sentence again. "Never assume that someone sees the light at the end of their struggle." If the idea hasn't stuck yet, stop reading here and read that sentence over and over again until it feels self-evident! It may very well be one of the most important sentences I ever write.

The sentence comes from places of deep pain in my life, as I have been watching my family and friendship circles get ripped apart by drug overdose and suicide for as long as I can remember. I was barely in 10th grade when I started burying people close to me, and since then, I have lost twelve people to these horrific and pervasive epidemics.

I understand that these issues are complicated and multi-faceted, and the circumstances in each scenario are as unique as the individuals involved. That being said, at times, these tragedies often have common story elements, and after years of tragedy, patterns start to emerge. Of all of the patterns I've seen, there are three that have stood out to me more than any other.

One of the gravest mistakes we make as human beings is to trivialize the experiences and trials other people are going through. I believe we trivialize primarily because we only see the surfaces of others' lives, which makes appreciating just how deep their struggles are difficult.

Personally, when I have lost friends to suicide, there has not been a single instance where I saw it coming or had true appreciation for just how bad things had gotten. Because of that, I will always wonder if I could have been more attentive, more active, or more involved in their lives and possibly done something to help them. These thoughts manifest as guilt that I carry with me daily.

The next mistake I believe we have a tendency to make is that we tend to diminish the weight others are carrying, especially if they are struggling with something we tend to manage deftly or something that we can't relate to. Because we can't relate to the burdens they carry, we can accidentally, or worse, intentionally put pressure on them to "man up" and bear the burden as we do.

To bring this to life a little bit, consider when two basketball players hit the court for a game of one-on-one. Though they are unique individuals, they bring with them two similar skill sets. Similarly, if we put two all-star football linemen together, the direct comparisons would be obvious and appropriate. Now switch the occasion and put a lineman in a one-on-one basketball game, or drop the power forward into a running-back position, and you can easily predict the calamity and injuries that are likely to ensue.

In both cases, rewarding the winners or judging the losers would be idiotic. In life, everyone is playing their own game and has developed different coping skills, strengths, and weaknesses as well as their own resiliencies. Because people are different and dealing with their own struggles, trivializing what someone else is going through is never helpful and only further damages the resilience of the person you are actually trying to help.

The final pattern I want to draw attention to is that, while we often consider ourselves to be champions for the people, we are responsible for, we are not always masters at sharing what we see in them and for them out loud. Unfortunately, I am as guilty of failing to share my vision with anyone else. As a consummate under-communicator, telling people how I feel is not something that comes easily to me in my personal life. The consequence is that my family often fails to understand how much they mean to me, how much potential I believe they have, or how bright the potential future I see so clearly for them is. It is a brutal reality that if you leave unchecked will deprive the people you care about of one of the things they need most of all: clear vision!

Lack of vision is one of three things that can cause people to fall into what we call the "Pit of Despair," a place that victims of tragedy often call home. If you asked me to describe it in one word, the first word that would come to mind would be dark. Give me another word, and I would say deep. It's a deep dark pit that can be virtually impossible to extricate yourself from without help.

The Pit of Despair is a term used to describe the feeling you have when you are near rock bottom and are all but ready to give up. It can be concerning a task, a skill, or even a relationship. People in the Pit of Despair hear that inner voice whispering sinisterly that "you will never be good enough," "you're a failure," or "you're unlovable." The worst part is that the Pit of Despair isn't confined to tasks and jobs at the office. It can easily originate from or creep into any relationship or activity we participate in.

At its worst, the Pit of Despair causes people to give up on jobs, give up on relationships, and sometimes even give up on life. While navigating The Pit of Despair is never foolproof, and

The Leader's Garden

we can never be everything to everyone, there is a simple set of principles that makes us more effective at serving those struggling. In fact, the same principles I am sharing that help grow healthy people (Time, Vision, and Encouragement) are the same I share with military commanders, chaplains, and mental health professionals when equipping them to do their part in the suicide and mental health epidemic we face.

When it comes to getting out of the pit, our first tool, Time, is crucial. It takes time to climb, and it takes effort to pull yourself up! Often, the worse the damage, the more time it takes to fix it. But Vision, Vision is where the real magic happens. Symbolically speaking, Vision is both the ladder and the candle that lights the way. Vision shows those we love and those we're responsible for that there's a path for them and that there is a brighter future! As we think of Vision, it is not a one-size-fits-all buzzword. It's important that we once again break it down into two pieces: Short-term Vision and Long-term Vision. Both are necessary as they provide different things.

Short-term Vision relates to the current situation and provides immediate clarity and hope. Imagine a player dropping a pass during a football game. At that moment, the coach can justify yelling and screaming, throwing things, and talking about all the wasted time spent training. Or, and this takes intentionality, he can remind the player that he believes in him and affirm his belief in the player's potential to catch the next one! We have all watched countless replays of both scenarios, but only one reflects the type of leader we should all aspire to be!

Long-term Vision moves past the immediate situation and focuses on the desired end-state. It provides perspective and helps us see beyond today, focusing instead on the person or situation that can be. In the football scenario, that may be focusing on the Superbowl ring, an MVP trophy, or a lucrative contract after a solid rookie year.

Understanding Vision and how to invest it in the short and long term is critical to growing healthy, high-performing people and helping those that are nearing rock bottom. For the latter, Time and Vision can be the difference between them fighting through to the end or throwing in the towel. One of the greatest regrets of my life is not telling the people I cared about most just how much they meant to me and just how much potential I saw in them. In the end, the lesson I have learned and have tried to intentionally pass on to my children is to never miss an opportunity to vocalize the best part of what you see in another human being.

CHAPTER 8
Where To?

Kevin had every intention of heading back to work that day and pouring vision into Eric's life, but nothing ever went according to plan, and it was almost a week later before he had time to sit and truly collect his thoughts. Embarrassingly, Eric's poor performance was driving the conversation again rather than Kevin's desire to be intentional. The good news was that Eric was making it into work; the bad news was that he was continually running late to meetings, he had failed to turn a proposal into a customer on time, and while he was physically there, he just wasn't present.

A short while later, the two men were seated in Kevin's office well into a conversation about Eric's life and his performance.

"Eric, I understand. I know this is hard, and we want to support you. We want to be there for you, both Julie and I. We want to help you, but it feels like you need time more than anything right now. I know you're low on vacation days, but we could do time off without pay or use some sick days if we have to.

"You say that you and Kyree want to work this out. Can we

help you find a good marriage counselor? Maybe you could do couples therapy. Do you think she would go with you?"

He was clutching at straws and wasn't really sure what to do. His own marriage wasn't exactly in perfect health, so at the moment, he felt he was trying to give away something he just didn't possess—which meant he was coming up short on ideas. Kevin looked at the notepad in his hands and ran the pen over the paper, hoping an idea would pop off the page.

Thankfully, Eric picked up the conversation, saving Kevin from his struggle. "Look, I appreciate it. I am sure Kyree does too. Truly." He paused before continuing, "It's just...My marriage isn't working out, I'm letting you down, and I'm even letting the team down now, which is a first. This isn't me. This isn't who I am. I'm dependable...I was dependable. I don't even recognize myself anymore, do you?"

Eric looked up, locking eyes with Kevin, seemingly looking for some glimpse of validation.

Kevin tried to respond, but he found it hard to formulate his thoughts, the weight of the situation and Eric's words pressing down on each of them, the pressure only building as the silence persisted.

Finally, Eric pushed through it, albeit with a soft voice, "Maybe I should just quit and make it easier on you. Make it easier on everyone else. Maybe it would be better for everyone if I just wasn't here anymore."

Eric leaned forward in his chair. He rested his elbows on his legs and his head on his hands.

Kevin's heart filled with despair, rage, frustration, and compassion all at once. He felt his chest tighten, and he wanted more than anything to chastise the man for trying to throw in the towel. He wanted to strangle Eric into seeing himself for the person he truly was, but for possibly the first time in his life, he held his tongue and used the sheer weight of his will to push the negative feelings down.

As he tried to process what he was hearing, a tiny voice grew increasingly louder. It was the voice of an elderly gardener, and it was repeating the same words over and over again. *Where there is no vision, the people perish...Where there is no vision, the people perish...Where there is no vision, the people perish...*The intensity coalesced into a single ray of focus, and Kevin's words were flowing from his mouth before he realized he was talking.

Kevin slammed his notebook down on the desk with the force of his epiphany. "Eric, you are going to get through this, and we are not going to give up on you. I know that you believe that Kyree loves you, and that means you can get through this. Sure, it's going to be a tough road, but you're tough, Eric. I've never known you to be a quitter. Even when it feels like hope is lost, there is always something you can do, and I know you are a fighter."

Kevin surprised himself, his inner voice almost speaking out loud, *There's always something you can do? Whose words are these?* Still, he kept on, "You're a fighter, and I know that you are not going to give up, no matter what."

Kevin drew a breath and then continued. "And we are not going to give up on you, either. Besides, I'm counting on you. I have plans for you. You have more potential than you realize, and this business, this company is depending on you for its future. You're the best project manager, the best team lead we've got. Your team loves you, they're committed to you. Heck, there may even be a chance for you to take my place at the head someday."

Eric's head was now up, and he was looking at Kevin. "I'm surprised to hear you say all of that."

Kevin smiled. "You mean a lot to me, to the team, and to your family. You can get through this, Eric. It's tough right now. I know it. You feel like you're in a pit. It's dark, and it's deep, and you can't see your way out. That's how it works. But you can do this, you can get yourself out of there, and if it's what you want, you can fix your family. You can do it if you want it badly enough and if you're willing to put in the work. We believe in you. I believe in you, and we're not going to give up on you. You're going to get through this, and I'm here to help you."

The words weren't elegant. They were more than a little redundant, and they weren't a cure-all, but they were sincere, and that shone through. They had an immediate impact, and there was a visible difference in Eric's demeanor. Eric adjusted himself and sat up just a little bit straighter.

"Yeah. Maybe you're right. I don't know. I don't really know where to start. Where to begin..." Eric trailed off.

"I'll tell you what. Julie gave me a list of a few couples therapists to call. Why don't you take the rest of the day off and give a few of these folks a call, see if any of them are taking new clients. Maybe they can start coaching you through the next few days. How's that sound?"

Eric managed half a smile, though it was obviously painful for him. "Good. It sounds good."

He stood up and nodded at Kevin, "Thanks, Boss, for everything," then turned towards the door and walked out.

Eric left Kevin alone to ponder what had just happened. Truly, he was shocked at just how impactful his words had been. It had all happened so quickly, and yet he had given Eric hope, possibly the most powerful of all human emotions. He wasn't sure if this would stick or just what impact it was going to have, but he had kept his word, and he was going to fight for Eric's best no matter the cost.

====

Later that night, riding the high of the day, Kevin was ready to pour vision into Anthony, but instead he found the house in turmoil. Whatever had happened before he walked in was quickly hitting a crescendo, as he heard Julie yelling after their son, "Anthony, go to your room until your father gets home!"

From the sound of things, Anthony was already at least halfway there, slamming his bedroom door just as Julie finished the sentence. Kevin thought about slinking back to the car and calling in late for dinner, but it was a passing thought, and he knew there was no turning back now.

"Hey," he said casually as he strolled into the dining room, pretending he had missed the bulk of what had just happened.

"Hey yourself," Julie shot back curtly with misdirected venom.

"Whoa!" Kevin held his hands up. "I'm not your enemy! Not this time, at least. Talk to me."

Julie just stared at him, clearly swelling with unreleased frustration that was looking for somewhere to land.

"Are you sure?" she said a little less enthusiastically, which Kevin felt was a huge step in the right direction.

Kevin decided not to react negatively to her frustrations and instead tried to be helpful. "What's going on, Julie? What happened?"

"Your son," Julie said, rising up and giving Kevin a fairly tense hug. "His history teacher called, said he was a great student, blah blah blah, but that he has been turning in work late, and today he had an important assignment due and he didn't turn it in at all. No excuse, no alibi, nothing."

"What?" Kevin's look of concern, even frustration, rivaled Julie's.

"I know, right? So I asked him about it, and you caught the tail end of that. I still have no idea what's going on. He got defensive, shut down, and now he's up there, waiting for whatever trouble you're going to bring him."

"I see," Kevin said, absolutely torn as to what to do. His instinct was to go upstairs and drag answers out of Anthony. He would apply pressure, push his son with words until he got what he wanted. Force Anthony to explain himself, to justify his actions, to apologize to his mother. It's what Kevin was best at, what he had always done.

This time, however, he watched the whole thing play out in his mind. He would go upstairs, he would yell, and Anthony would shut down, comply, and fix today's problem, but more and more relationship cords would be cut…possibly the last few still hanging on. He saw it all happen with such clarity that it may as well have been a documentary live on TV.

Somehow he knew that if he walked up those stairs and

unloaded on his son, it would be the final cut in their relationship.

"Julie, I..." he paused, clarifying his thoughts. "Julie, I love you. I want to help. But I don't want to yell. I don't want to chastise him. I want to try something, something different."

Julie looked up at him with a quizzical look on her face. She cocked her head slightly but didn't say a word.

"Look. I believe in Anthony, and I know you do too. He is a good kid, a forgetful kid, but a good one. I want to surprise him, and rather than go up there and read him the riot act, I just want to love on him and pour some vision into him. It's like in Proverbs 29—where there is no vision, the people perish. I think Anthony might be perishing because he doesn't see himself the way we do, and even if that's not the whole problem, it's at least part of it. Our part...well, my part."

Julie looked inquiringly at Kevin. "Where is all this coming from?"

"Julie, I'm sorry. I've gotten this so wrong, and I have to start making it right, right now."

Julie nodded. "Ok."

She went from her tense posture to giving Kevin a long, affectionate hug. While Kevin knew that there were so many conversations they still needed to have, and there was still so much to work on, today Kevin was ready to count her warm affection as a HUGE win!

As they ended the hug, she said, "Good luck, buddy," and gave him a flash of the playful half-smile that had played no small part in him falling madly in love with her so many years ago.

Kevin, again stunned at just how well Frank's principles were working, turned and headed towards the stairs.

==========The Big Idea==========

Time and Vision are critical pieces of both our preventative and reactive toolkits that can be used in virtually every encounter we have with other human beings. All that being said, knowing the principles, even believing that they work, is not enough.

Knowledge without application is just theory, and while theory has a crucial place, we must always be doers and not simply hearers. On top of that, I would add that you have to fight the urge to get complacent when things feel easy, and always remember that resilience is built in between the challenges we encounter, not during!

==========Exercise==========

In the last chapter, you identified at least one person in your life that is going through an internal or external struggle. Considering that person:

1. What is one practical thing you can do to help that person with the problem he or she is having?
2. What Short-term Vision can you share with that person?
3. Schedule time this week to offer that help or speak life to that Vision.

CHAPTER 8
Reflection

"Knowledge is useless without consistent application." Julian Hall

So far in this book, I have hammered home one idea and hit on two applications. The idea I have been trying to get you to understand is that caring for people is a skill, not a personality trait, and that skills can be taught.

After that, I taught you that Time (Formal and Informal) and Vision (Short-term and Long-term) are crucial components to taking care of people and must be implemented immediately, no matter where you currently are in your relationships.

I do not want this book to be something you reflect on and never take action on, and I hope that these practical applications are already impacting the relationships in your life. If they are not, remember, knowledge without action is not, will not, and cannot ever be enough. You must continue to fill your toolbox with practical tools and make a plan to use them, and that plan must include steps you are going to take TODAY.

Everything we've worked through so far, if applied, has the potential to make you a better parent or spouse tonight AND a better leader in the workplace tomorrow. The concepts are simple, and they are easy to implement, meaning they can be taught at will to anyone stuck sitting next to you on a bus or airplane! Teach these concepts to the people you know!

If you are dealing with damaged relationships, or if people in your life are struggling to find their value, spend time with them and speak Vision into their lives. Don't wait, don't overthink, just do it! Even if it's awkward, you will get better over time. You will learn what works and what doesn't, and your skills will improve, but only if you put what you learn into practice and obsessively fight for the best in those you lead.

The Leader's Garden

CHAPTER 9

Turn Up the Heat

"Well, tell me your stories," Frank said, leaning against the boulder that Kevin though should surely have his name etched into it.

The day was hot, much hotter than usual, and though Frank always seemed excited to see Kevin, today he seemed more rushed and uncomfortable than usual, likely due to the heat.

"Where to start..." Kevin began, showing more discomfort than Frank in no small part due to the slacks and long sleeves he was wearing. The heat was already taking a toll on him.

"I really think we're having some breakthroughs, Frank. I mean, I never would have predicted this a few months ago, but I feel like I have a chance to save my marriage and pull everything together at work."

Frank affirmed him, "Mm-hmm. I'd say so. Let's walk and talk."

He led Kevin in a direction they hadn't gone before, back towards the warehouse area.

"Sure." Kevin smiled, following beside Frank. "Where was I? Oh yeah, Anthony's still struggling. It's probably getting worse, to be honest. But there is something there, something under the surface. I see it budding." He looked around the nursery. "No pun intended, of course."

"Of course," Frank replied, wincing at the humor.

"A few days ago, he botched it pretty bad at school and probably would have dropped himself a whole letter grade if he hadn't gotten some extra credit work."

Frank turned up an eyebrow. "I see. So, what'd you do?"

It was an obvious challenge; a test of all Kevin had been learning. As he spoke, they made their way around the building to a truck piled high with mulch bags. Without hesitating, Frank grabbed a bag and walked it over to a small pile someone had started earlier. Kevin's eyes widened as he realized what was about to happen.

Frank paused and made eye contact with Kevin, who immediately stated, "You can't be serious."

A bag of mulch slung over his shoulder, Frank replied with an ear-to-ear grin, "Oh, yes I can. These bags aren't going to unload themselves, you know. Let's get to work."

For a few minutes, Kevin and Frank put the conversation on hold as they worked to establish a rhythm. Frank was obviously in shape for his age. Though well-worn, he was still incredibly capable of lifting the bags of mulch deftly and tossing them onto the pile with ease. Sure, Frank moved slower than he probably used to, but honestly, with Kevin's sedentary lifestyle, Frank was keeping pace and outworked the younger man. In fact, now that Kevin thought about it, Frank wasn't breathing half as hard as he was, which was even more evident when Frank picked the conversation back up again.

"So, what did you do when Anthony messed up?"

Kevin had to choose his words carefully since his lungs were working hard to keep pace with the hot air and hard work. "Well, I wanted to go up there and let him have it, Frank. Especially after the way he and his mother were having it out, but I surprised everyone, myself most of all, I think. It might sound silly, but for a minute, it was like you were there in the room with me."

He tossed another bag of mulch onto the pile, pausing to take a few breaths, his hands on his hips. "Every time I even thought about going upstairs, I heard your voice in my head, and I knew if I went up there and let loose on him, it would probably be the last time he truly tried to hear me ever again. I've gotten it wrong so many times."

While Kevin paused, Frank just kept at his work, methodically walking back and forth, causing Kevin to shake his head and get back to work.

Kevin tried to push through and keep the conversation moving forward. "I know when I walked in his room, he was expecting the end of the world, but instead I started with the world's most awkward hug and told him it was going to be alright, that we would sort this out."

"I see," Frank said, "and...how did it all turn out?"

"I mean," Kevin paused, "about as good as can be expected, I guess. We didn't leave the room hating each other, which is a great start. But seriously, he apologized to his mother, which was a great step. And the next day, he worked things out with his teacher somehow and got permission to turn in his work late if he did some extra credit work."

Kevin paused for quite a while, falling into the rhythmic cycle of grabbing bags off the truck and tossing them onto the pile, almost keeping in time with Frank at this point. Eventually though, his shirt was soaked through.

Kevin said, "Alright Frank, I get it. You're in better shape than me! Can we take a break for a minute?"

Frank, now carrying a bag of mulch over each shoulder, just smiled at Kevin.

"Boy do I still have a lot to teach you, letting an old man put you to shame out here. Lucky your family's not here to see this," Frank joked.

Truthfully though, Kevin saw through Frank's friendly bravado. He had been noticing him slowing down and breathing a little faster the last few rounds and knew some water would do them both some good. Fortunately, there was a cooler right by

The Leader's Garden

them, and Frank encouraged Kevin to help himself.

Water in hand, the two of them leaned back against the wall and looked at the truck, which was now at least two-thirds empty.

Frank then stated flatly, "Shame I'm going to have you load those bags back up on the truck after you finish that water bottle."

Kevin's heart nearly stopped beating until he realized Frank was having fun at his expense. They shared a laugh, and then, downing the last of the water, they fell back into a rhythm again, quickly emptying the last of the truck.

As they finished, Frank started to get some of his vigor back. "Well, it sounds like you've got it all figured out, then. Well done."

Though Kevin sensed Frank was sincere, he wasn't convinced their lessons were over, not by a longshot.

"I know none of this is a cure-all. I mean, I don't expect to undo all of my mistakes in a night. But, somehow, I feel like it's just a matter of time, you know? Like, if I can just hold back that inner voice of mine and be intentional for a little while, nothing will ever be the same," he said.

"Well, I'd certainly hope not, young man," Frank said with a smile, but it was the smile of one who had once had and lost. It was the smile of fond memories rather than current joy. "Nothing will ever be the same. That's pretty much life's only guarantee. We can predict with some certainty what tomorrow will be like, but beyond a few more tomorrows, things get pretty unpredictable."

Leading Kevin to a faucet, Frank began washing his hands and beckoned Kevin to do the same.

"But enough about that," Frank said. "Tell me about the other one, about work."

Kevin paused, thinking while he washed and dried his hands, which were not accustomed to being this dirty. "Well, what can I say? Eric's a good man..."

Frank tossed his paper towels into a trash can. "Don't waste my time now, I know he's a good man. We're all good men," he said with a little mischief. "I want to hear about the living, breathing man. Who is Eric?"

Kevin took the challenge in stride. "Right. Well, I'm not giving up, Frank, I'll tell you that much. His life, his marriage, they are falling apart. I never realized just how hard this company has been on all of us. I never realized the toll on my house and theirs.

"I'm trying to get him some help. Julie and I are going full-court press, and I'm pouring vision into his life just like you said I should. I'm trying to do it daily too, even if it doesn't always work out." He paused, then continued. "I believe his best, his family's best, is here where we understand him, and where we can make his family a priority."

"And he knows this?" Frank asked, eyeing a nearby trash can that was about to overflow.

He made his way over, pulled the bag out, and tied it up with Kevin trailing behind.

"He knows this, even if he doesn't believe it yet," Kevin said, offering help, which Frank brushed off.

"Vision," Frank said matter-of-factly.

"Vision," Kevin replied.

"Well, there's nothing left but to keep that up, then. You write that vision down, you refine it, you memorize it, and you repeat it out loud, both to Anthony and to Eric—and to yourself, for that matter. Never lose sight of who this is really about, and I think you've got a fighting chance of pulling both of them through this."

He hoisted the trash bag over his shoulder and started walking back towards the dumpster, which, even after this long, made Kevin feel awkward for not helping.

If Frank noticed, there was no indication, as he just continued on. "You've done good so far. Real good. Better than I expected. You're fighting for their best even when it isn't easy. You're reining in your passion when faced with a challenge, and you're seeing the fruit.

"You deserve praise, high praise. And, you've got mine, son. You're certainly earning it. I'm proud of you, and I don't say that lightly."

Kevin wasn't looking at Frank when he talked, in no small part because this type of praise made him mildly uncomfortable.

Frank must have realized this because he repeated himself, but this time with more force, "I'm proud of you. You hear me?"

"I hear you," Kevin said apologetically. "I hear you, Frank. Thank you, it means...It means a lot—"

"Listen," Frank continued, cutting him off as they arrived at the dumpster. "Can you get that lid for me? Thanks. Now, where was I? Oh yes, you've made mistakes. You've let your priorities get all out of whack, and you've messed with the lives of people around you, people you care about.

"But you listen, and you listen good. You're not a mistake. You aren't the problem. You've made some bad choices, but you're manning up and doing something about them because you're a man of character, a man, a leader worth following, and I am proud to call you my friend."

This time, Kevin didn't let his tendency to feel uncomfortable dominate him. Instead, he felt pride at earning Frank's praise. Truly, he was speechless and happy to take that feeling in.

Then, in typical Frank fashion, he said, "But you're not done yet. You've still got a few things to learn, my boy, and your next lesson starts now."

Leaving the dumpster behind, he didn't wait for Kevin to catch up but just kept on talking.

"I told you there were three things you had to do well to take care of people. The first was time, formal and informal. The second was vision, short-term and long-term. Here you are, rambling on, and you haven't even asked me about the third one.

"Only God knows how many of these sessions we have left, son. I'm not getting any younger, and if you don't buy something from me soon, we're both getting banned from the property," he said with a chuckle, which Kevin returned.

Frank continued, "Look, you've already gotten a small taste of number three without realizing it. First, with your son and Eric, and even a little today with me.

"You've watched your son change his behavior without you even asking him to because both plants and people grow towards the sunlight. They grow towards nourishment, and unlike plants, people need more than just water, nutrients, and sunlight. They also need encouragement.

"Without realizing it, you've been sowing seeds of encouragement into everything you've been doing, but now it's time to get intentional about it, just like I've been with you. Look at our conversation today. Not only did I validate you by telling you that you're not a problem and that you're a good man, but I also took the things I've seen, the things you've done, and I forced you to see them through my eyes.

"When we're in the thick of it, our brains force us to look at the next problem so we can produce the next solution. We often move the goalpost before we score the goal, preventing ourselves from appreciating the progress we've made! That's why it's critical, crucial even, that people see themselves through someone else's eyes. We must ENCOURAGE the people around us by showing them how much they mean to us and how valuable their efforts really are, especially when they're in the Pit of Despair.

"And hear me well here. Encouraging people based on accomplishments is necessary, but it isn't nearly enough. If you focus solely on their accomplishments, then your relationship is transactional at best. They'll always feel that your approval comes only through their accomplishments and not their humanity. You with me so far?"

Kevin nodded, listening but also remembering times he had gotten this wrong.

"Mmm-hmm," Frank said skeptically, but continued on anyway. "The third piece, the capstone to all of this, is encouragement. Like always, there are two kinds: encouragement of performance and encouragement of the person.

"You've got to make a list of their accomplishments, check it twice, and let them know they've done good when they have. But you also have to validate their humanity and their worth as human beings by sharing how much you value them and what they mean to you. If THEY don't matter to YOU or don't know how much they matter to you, well...then what does any of this count for?"

He paused, scanning Kevin's face for understanding.

"I got it...I mean, I get it. At least, I think I do," Kevin replied, "but I'm not going to lie...This one is tough. Look at Eric. He's falling behind. He's failing. It's not going well. How am I supposed to encourage him without it coming across as fake? I mean, he knows he's not killing it."

Frank nodded along slowly as if he'd anticipated the question before it was vocalized.

"You ever take your son bowling when he was little? I mean, really little?" Frank asked.

Kevin nodded.

"How'd he does?" Frank asked.

"Not good. I mean, good for his age, I guess," Kevin replied.

"And did you just give him a 12-pound ball and have him chuck it down the lane?" Frank quizzed.

"No, we put up bumpers and used this ball ramp that let him set his ball down and give it a push, and even then, he only usually hit one or two pins. He was young," Kevin said with a smile, remembering the times he had spent with the little guy.

"Yeah, I got that," Frank continued, "and I'm betting when he hit a couple pins, you and your wife celebrated with him like he got strikes and spares, am I right?"

"Oh, you're right," Kevin laughed, starting to see where this was going.

"Encouragement's a funny thing, Kevin. Sometimes we reserve it for the good days, the big accomplishments. We often feel like it's for home runs and touchdowns...but we can forget that home runs and touchdowns are different for all of us, and sometimes they are far more about where we are and what we are going through TODAY than how tough any particular project or task is.

"We high five the young ones when they hit a pin because we want them to keep trying. We point out small wins in small children so they grow TOWARDS that sunlight. They want our approval. It's all they want most days.

"The big secret, I think, is that that doesn't fade with childhood. We all want to know that we are valued, that our efforts aren't unnoticed, and that we matter. In fact, I'd say the deeper and darker our Pit of Despair is, the MORE encouragement we need. My guess is, and this isn't condemnation, that you've been, until now, the type of person that gives huge high fives to those that earn them but expect people to pull their weight before they get praise."

Kevin confirmed Frank's thoughts with a nod.

"Well, that stops now, today," Frank continued. "We're going to start with Anthony and Eric, but that's just the beginning. Starting right now, you're going to make a list of ways to encourage them and validate their worth daily, and on top of that, you're going to hunt for daily opportunities to validate something they've done. You think you can do that?"

"Yeah, I think so," Kevin said, though a little skepticism lingered.

"Yeah, well. I've got one more secret for you," Frank continued. "Sometimes, you've got to make stuff up."

Kevin, caught by surprise, blurted out, "What?"

Frank put a hand up, backtracking a bit. "Oh, I don't mean you lie. But I do mean to be intentional about setting people up for success so they have an environment where they can grow and thrive. Sometimes, we have to set people up for high fives by giving them something to do that we know they can accomplish. Something that takes effort but we know they won't fail at. We can build up their confidence slowly over time by letting them knock over a single bowling pin just to encourage them in that. Then, over time, as they carry a heavier load and build on their skills and confidence, we remove the bumpers, and the high fives only come with 5 pins and eventually just strikes and spares.

"But those are in the good times, when we have the luxury of being proactive. When folks are in the Pit of Despair, encouragement needs to be heavy, and it needs to be often."

Kevin stood in stunned silence. The concepts seemed so crystal clear to him. He had always viewed encouragement as a tool in his toolbox but one that was used to reward superior performance. *How have I never seen this?* The idea of using encouragement to foster growth and bring people back to confidence was mind-blowing to him.

"You feel like you have something to take action on this week?" Frank asked matter-of-factly.

"I do, Frank. I really do," Kevin replied, surprised he had taken so much from today.

"Good, then get out of here so I can get under some real shade!"

With that, Frank stood up and offered Kevin a solid handshake.

==========Exercise===========

Consider your work/family relationships. Are there any people that need encouragement due to their circumstances or because they are building a new skill set? If so, commit to accomplishing the following:

1. At the end of each day this week, look for one thing they have done that you can acknowledge verbally.

2. At least once this week, spend a few minutes with them sharing something about them that you admire, something about them that is unique, or something about them that is special.

CHAPTER 9
Reflection

"Don't ever be too busy to encourage others" Unknown

A trend that started in the '90s, during my teenage years, is commonly referred to as the "participation trophy." Believe me, as I sit in my local coffee shop, I can almost hear your collective groans. Suppose you've been living under a rock. In that case, the "participation trophy" refers to the idea that each of us should receive accolades for the work that we contribute, even if the work we contribute isn't worthy of commendation. Another way to say it is that even losers still get trophies.

Now, I will be the first to stand up and say that giving losers trophies is likely not sending the right message. As you are probably well aware, in the real world, in the business world, there truly is no such thing as a participation trophy, so raising a generation with that expectation seems foolhardy. For better or worse, in the real world, accolades and praise are given only to solid performers and sometimes not even then, unfortunately. While I believe accolades should be both rare and well-earned, we have to learn to separate awards, which are rare, from encouragement and make the latter a part of our daily routine!

Accolades and rewards, such as trophies, are appropriate when significant accomplishments are achieved. On the other hand, encouragement is as essential to human development as sunlight is to the growth of fruits and vegetables. As leaders, all too often, we treat our encouragement as currency and use it transactionally to reward good behavior or strong performance without realizing that those in our organizations that are struggling the most, languishing in bottomless pits, are the ones who need our encouragement the most.

Like Time and Vision, Encouragement must be dispensed generously. For those we are fortunate enough to care for, encouragement serves as a reminder that we haven't given up on them and validates that their hard work is being noticed.

The one thing I feel like I must say here is that I understand that hard work alone doesn't pay the bills. It is entirely possible for our people to work incredibly hard and still fail to meet performance standards! I am often challenged on Encouragement in ways I am not on Time and Vision because people often feel that encouraging someone that is not at their peak will somehow reinforce bad behavior or outright waste their time. Never forget that encouragement does not cancel out the requirement for accountability. They go hand in hand, and accountability is always non-negotiable.

With that out of the way, when it comes to both Encouragement and accountability, we should understand where the person we are leading is, how much time we have to work with them, and where we reasonably expect them to be by the end of our time together. Like my daughters at the bowling alley, some people need encouragement for knocking down a single pin if we expect them to enthusiastically try again. Just waking up in the morning is a significant accomplishment for people deep in the Pit of Despair. For others, like my teenagers, who only expect a fist bump but aren't looking for high-five parties unless they hit that strike or spare, encouragement can be less frequent and less enthusiastic when it comes to small wins.

Make no mistake, there are times when we are rebuilding confidence in others and have to set them up for small wins, giving them tasks we know they can complete just to encourage them on the back end.

So, to make this a little more practical, imagine you have two jars full of Encouragement, and part of your daily routine is to pour those jars out until there is absolutely none left. Don't worry; they refill with every new day!

The first jar of Encouragement is your performance jar. This jar is the one you use to tell people you see what they are doing. This jar should be used liberally, especially when you notice people are diligent, faithful, or going just a few steps beyond their typical behavior. This first jar can also be used any time you see someone living out your organizational values! Remember, people grow towards sunlight, and people will start growing towards your encouragement, just wait and see.

The second jar is drastically different from the first jar. The first jar is performance-based, but the second jar is for validation! I use this second jar with my 18-year-old son when I tell him how glad I am that we are friends. It's the jar I use when I tell my wife how grateful I am that she is in my life. I pull this jar out any time I tell people how awesome they are, how lucky we are to have them, or why they are so valuable to the team.

Endeavoring to validate the humanity and innate worth of the people around us is critical to their healthy growth and infinitely more so if they struggle to see a better future. The internet is full of stories of people ready to end their lives only to change their minds on encountering a single dose of validation in the form of encouragement. I often tell my children to never miss an opportunity to tell someone they are doing a good job. I model this wherever we go and consistently pour encouragement (both performance and validation) any and everywhere I can.

I don't do it for any reason other than to leave a positive impact wherever I go. That being said, the return I receive is dramatic. Virtually daily, I am blessed with free things, front-of-the-line access, or some other unwarranted perk simply because I made people feel better about themselves sincerely and authentically. A few seconds ago, almost as if on cue, one of the baristas just walked over and asked if I would like a free cookie. It has gotten to the point that my children call it "pulling a dad" when they make someone feel special and receive some bonus in return.

If I can have this much impact on total strangers, how much more can you impact the people in your life that truly value what you have to say? If you decide to implement the "never miss a chance to tell someone they're doing a good job" policy in your family, I would love to hear your experiences and the impact they have on you and your family. You can send them to me at book@marktilsher.com!

EPILOGUE

Several months had passed since Kevin had started meeting weekly with the unlikeliest of mentors, and tonight—tonight was something a little different for his family. Tonight, Frank was visiting them in their home and was resting in a comfortable chair after having spent the evening sharing stories, playing games, and laughing, often at Kevin's expense.

Julie and Anthony had grown increasingly fond of Frank, and he had become a weekly dinner guest in the home the last few weeks.

"Frank, we're so happy you let us celebrate your birthday with you," Julie said warmly.

"Yeah, Mr. Frank," Anthony followed up, "we're happy you're here."

"Oh, now," Frank chastised them, "I told you all, I don't need a fuss."

His words were obviously all bluster. From their talks, Kevin knew that it had been a long time since Frank had any family nearby, and he had watched him lower his guard more and more lately, seemingly open to integrating himself into their family.

Kevin smiled and reached under his chair, retrieving a

The Leader's Garden

medium-sized box wrapped with green ribbon.

"We got you something, Frank...for your birthday," he said clumsily.

Frank, surprised, shot back, "Oh no, really, you shouldn't have..."

This time, his voice quivered uncharacteristically, and the words came out much slower.

"I know, Frank. Still, open it; it's from all of us." Kevin beamed.

Kevin handed the package gingerly to Frank, who took it with both hands, hands that trembled ever so slightly.

Frank sat in silence, holding the package quietly for several long seconds. Then, his hands began moving slowly, one of his fingers tracing the green lace. Frank seemed to be lost in time for a moment, as if he had forgotten they were even there.

"Open it, Mr. Frank!" Anthony prodded impatiently.

Frank responded, seeminging to snap out of some memory, "Ok, ok. This might be the last present I ever get. Now, let me enjoy the moment!"

He smiled. Gently, Frank pulled the strings on the green bow and lifted the box. What was inside made him gasp audibly.

The box contained a meticulously crafted holster that at first glance seemed to be right out of the Wild West. The belt was thick, 9oz saddle leather, cut flawlessly and conditioned to a lustrous sheen, with a wide silver buckle adorned with matching rivets. It was only on closer inspection that one would see this wasn't a gun holster at all. Instead, it was a gardening belt with two deep pockets perfect for holding gardening trawls and pruning shears.

"Frank," Julie asked softly, "do you like it?"

Frank was finally at a loss for words. His hands caressed the soft, durable leather as he stared at his own name etched across the belt.

"I...I don't know what to say," Frank muttered.

"Frank," Kevin said, his voice soothing and gentle, "you don't have to say anything. But there's more. Read the note."

Slowly, Frank reached into the box and found a small note.
Thank you for saving our family.
-- Kevin, Julie, & Anthony

As Frank stared at the note, Julie smiled kindness radiated from her eyes, "We wanted you to know how important you are, how important you've been to our family, to our marriage. We want you to be encouraged, Frank, every day when you wake up and put this on; we want you to know how important you've been to us, how much you mean to us."

"Yeah, Mr. Frank. We appreciate you...all you and my dad have been doing. It's like we're all different people—or at least on our way to it," Anthony added.

Frank smiled, but his gaze was firmly locked on Kevin, the two of them sharing a look of mutual admiration, respect, and gratitude.

======================

Things continued for Kevin and his family much like they had before. Kevin continued working, Anthony continued going to school, and Julie supported the family and managed their home.

Most people wouldn't have noticed that anything had changed from the outside, but inside their home, the more Kevin stayed faithful to pouring Time, Vision, and Encouragement into both Julie and Anthony, the closer their family got, and the longer the space between each conflict grew.

The changes at work were no different. While Eric and his wife continued working on their marriage, Eric's work performance began to increase dramatically as his home situation began dropping from DEFCON 4. Eric wasn't the only employee that experienced the benefits of Kevin's continued transformation, and over time, respect and connection in Kevin's closest relationships became the norm. Kevin never missed a chance to share how his life had turned around when he met a simple gardener named Frank.

==========Exercise===========

Considering the relationships in your team/family, the Pit of Despair, and Time, Vision, & Encouragement, answer the following questions:

1. What has changed most about the way you view your part in both growing healthy, high-performing people and serving those who are in The Pit of Despair?
2. Choose specific people, and write down the specific impact you believe implementing these principles faithfully would have in their lives.
3. Are there any areas where you have damaged relationships, or failed to provide the right mix of Time, Vision, and Encouragement to? If so, write those instances down and schedule a time to meet face to face and make it right.

EPILOGUE
Reflection

"What you plant now, you will harvest later." Og Mandino

We all know that Rome wasn't built in a day and that damaged people don't suddenly recover to full health overnight. That being said, people can and do change dramatically when their desire is coupled with the right combination of Time, Vision, and Encouragement from their leaders.

This book has been about demonstrating that leadership is less about how much we care than it is about how crucial demonstrating that care through practical techniques can be. It is also meant to demonstrate that these skills can be both taught and learned.

Kevin was a man with misplaced priorities surrounded by damaged people. Some he had hurt, and others he had inadvertently ignored to both his and their detriment. In all cases, his part to play was the same.

To nourish those around us, to grow healthy, high-performing people, you must be obsessively for them and never for yourself. You must be both intentional and incredibly liberal in heaping Time, Vision, and Encouragement on them. The only thing standing between you and the people that need you most are your inhibitions and other priorities. If this book has taught you anything, if it has caused you to reflect on even a single relationship in your life, then my only request is that you go out into the world and not only implement these simple principles but also teach them to others so that they can do the same.

Going forward, I encourage you to connect with me and the thousands of other leaders in our community striving to make a difference in the lives of those they lead. Now, go forward and join me in growing your own garden filled with healthy, high-performing people!

ACKNOWLEDGMENTS

To Mike Oppedahl, you are the man I want to be when I grow up. Thank you for liberating me and fighting for my best. There is no greater champion in all the earth.

To Jeremie Kubicek, thank you for your unwavering support. The way you lift as you climb is the purest form of mentorship I have ever seen in my life.

To Steve Cockram, thank you for your wisdom and guidance. Had we not had breakfast in London, I'm not sure I would have ever had the courage to move forward.

To Amber Mitchell, thank you for fighting for me for over a decade! You are tireless and relentless in your quest to serve our nation and its defenders. Thank you!

To Andrew Mathias, you changed the entire trajectory of my life. Thank you for treating me as a peer, and mentoring me into the Senior Non-Commissioned Officer I needed to be.

To Anne & Emma Davis, Thank you for your patience and

practical love! Thank you for taking part in this ministry effort with me, you are absolute ROCK stars!

To Ed Diaz, thank you for treating me as a friend and speaking the truth into my life. I value your friendship and apprenticeship.

To Edwin Ludwigsen, I have never been more grateful or intimidated to serve someone as with you, sir. Thank you for believing in me and allowing me in where I knew I didn't belong.

To Jeremy Huggins, from the moment I met you, you have been one of my greatest champions. Thank you for seeking to mentor me and continuing to check on me. When I am seemingly at my lowest, you are always there to check on me and lift me up!

To Joanne Bass, it broke my heart to tell you that I was retiring from the Air Force. Thank you for believing in me and allowing me to fight for your best and the best of our Airmen.

To K.C., I don't deserve you as a champion but am grateful for you and all you do for me and my family. I only wish we had more time together IN uniform!

To Phillip Easton, you will never know how much I owe you! Thank you for being my Chief, and Champion! I would follow you anywhere.

To Rob Joseph, you bring JOY to this fight, and it goes without saying I'm grateful for you. Watching you do your thing is life-giving and inspiring!

To Vaughan Moore, thanks for the partnership! The long nights and days, the wrestling through concepts and ideas, and the never-ending optimism! Excited for the future!!!

To my amazing book launch team, thank you for walking with me and bringing high support! Each of you has a special place in my heart:

Aaron Lee	Davis Carman	Kim Censabella	Shannon Sutton
Angela Tilsher	Ed Diaz	Kristine McReynolds	Skot Waldron
Brandon Hurley	Elaine Gard	Ladonna R. Abdullah	Teresa West
Brian Kluball	Jeremy Huggins	Montanna Young	Tracy Rader
Brianna Simpson	Josh Vanderbeck	Nikia Lettunich	Travis Wilkin
Carlos Castro	Joshua Vanegas	Nina Kemp	Vaughan Moore
Casey Smith	Kathi Glascock	Patrick Boudreau	Chasidy Sells
Kayla Kersey	Phillip Vana		

Made in the USA
Coppell, TX
03 August 2022